KT-503-303

SIXTY DEGREES NORTH

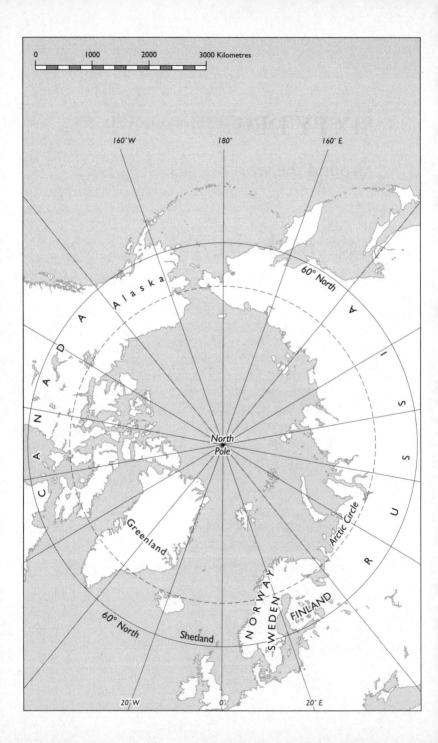

SIXTY DEGREES NORTH

around the world in search of home

Malachy Tallack

Polygon

First published in 2015 by Polygon, an imprint of
Birlinn Ltd
West Newington House
10 Newington Road
Edinburgh
EH9 1QS
www.birlinn.co.uk

Text © Malachy Tallack, 2015

Photographs © Malachy Tallack, 2015
except where otherwise noted

Extracts from *Sixty Degrees North* have previously been published in *Irish Pages*, *PN Review* and *Earthlines*

The right of Malachy Tallack to be identified as the author of this work has been asserted by him in accordance with the Copyright, Design and Patent Act 1988.

All rights reserved. No part of this publication may be reproduced, stored, or transmitted in any form, or by any means, electronic, photocopying, recording or otherwise, without the express written permission of the publishers.

9 8 7 6 5 4 3

ISBN: 978 1 84697 336 9

British Library Cataloguing in Publication Data
A catalogue record for this book is available from the British Library

Typeset in Sabon at Birlinn
Printed and bound by
CPI Group (UK) Ltd, Croydon, CR0 4YY

Contents

Illustrations

Maps

HOMEGOING

I can remember the day: silver-skied and heavy with rain. It was early winter and I had just turned seventeen. The morning had been spent in bed, sick and sleepless, but by lunchtime boredom made me move. I stood up and shuffled towards the window, pulling a dressing-gown around my shoulders. The house in which I spent my teenage years faced east over the harbour in Lerwick, Shetland's capital town. From my room on the second floor I could see out onto our little garden, with the green picnic bench and the wooden trellis set against a low stone wall. Beyond, I could see fishing boats at the pier, and the blue and white ferry that chugged back and forth to the island of Bressay, just across the water.

Shetland lies at sixty degrees north of the equator, and the world map on our kitchen wall had taught me that, if I could see far enough, I could look out from that window across the North Sea to Norway, and to Sweden, then over the Baltic to Finland, to St Petersburg, then Siberia, Alaska, Canada and Greenland. If I could see far enough, my eyes would eventually bring me back, across the Atlantic Ocean, to where I was standing. I thought about that journey as I looked out over the harbour, half-dressed and shivering. Though I'd never travelled anywhere at this latitude before, I imagined then that I could see those places from above. I felt myself carried around the parallel, lifted and dragged, as though connected to a wire. The world turned and I turned with it, circling from home towards home again until I reached, inevitably, the back of my own head. Dizziness rose through me like a gasp of bubbles, and I fainted, briefly, landing on my knees with a jolt on the bedroom floor. Exhausted, I hauled myself back up again and into bed, and there I fell asleep and dreamed my way once more around the parallel. That dream, that day, never left me.

A few months earlier, my father had died. He left me one morning beside a lake in Sussex, not far from where he lived, and I spent the hours that followed fishing beneath August sunshine. It was the kind of quiet, ordinary day on which nothing extraordinary ought to happen. But it did. By the time the afternoon rolled towards evening and I began to wonder why he had not returned, he was already dead – killed in a car crash on his way to visit my grandmother in hospital. Waiting there alone, I clung to hope for as long as I could, but I had already imagined the worst. And though eventually I walked away, in search of someone to tell me what had happened and somewhere I could spend the night, part of me was left there beside the lake. Part of me has never stopped waiting.

On that evening, all of the plans I had came to an end, and when I returned to Shetland the following week it was with nothing in front of me. My parents had separated years before, and while I lived with my mother and brother in the islands, my father was in the south of England, at the other end of the British Isles. That summer I had been offered a place to study music at a school of performing arts in South London, and so I went to live with my dad. I had found a direction and followed it. When he died, just before the first term began, that direction was lost forever. I had no choice but to go north again, and once there I had no idea what I would do. On the day I stood beside the window, dreaming of the parallel, I had been stranded for months, lost and half-hollowed by grief. I was looking for something certain. I was looking for a direction.

Over the years, Shetland has made much of its latitude. When I was at high school, our youth club was called 60

North. Later, there was a fishing industry newspaper with the same name. And a tourist radio station. And an online magazine. And a skip-hire company. And a beer, brewed in Lerwick.

Part of this ubiquity is down to a lack of imagination, and part of it to a kind of brand mentality: selling our northern exoticism, or something like that. But there is more to it, I think. Sixty degrees north is a story that we tell, both to ourselves and to others. It is a story about where – and perhaps also who – we are. 'Shetland is at the same latitude as St Petersburg,' tourists are informed, 'as Greenland, and Alaska'. And they are told this because it seems to mean something. It seems to mean more, for instance, than the fact that Shetland is at the same longitude as Middlesbrough, or as Ouagadougou. To be at sixty degrees north is to be connected to a world that is more interesting and more mysterious than the one to which the islands are usually bound. To highlight it is to assert that this is not just a forgotten corner of the British Isles; Shetland belongs also to something else, something bigger. Once it was at the geographical heart of a North Atlantic empire, enclosed within the Norse world in a way that provokes nostalgia even now, more than five hundred years after the islands were pawned by the king of Denmark and Norway to Scotland. Unlike political or cultural geographies, the sixtieth parallel is certain and resolute; it is impervious to the whims of history. Shetland belongs to the north, upon this line with no corners to which it may be consigned. At sixty degrees, Shetland is as central as anywhere and everywhere else.

But what of those other places on that list we recite to tourists? What do we share with them, beyond a latitude? What exactly is this club to which we so enthusiastically belong? Looking at a map, it is possible to claim that the sixtieth parallel is a kind of border, where the almost-north and the north come together. In Europe, it crosses the very top of the British Isles and the bottom of Finland, Sweden and Norway. The line skirts the lower tip of Greenland, and of South-central Alaska. It slices the great expanse of Russia in half, and in Canada it does the same, marking the official boundary between the northern territories and southern provinces. All along the parallel are regions whose inhabitants are challenged, to some extent, by the places in which they live. They are challenged by climate, by landscape, by remoteness. And yet those inhabitants choose to remain. They make their peace with the islands and the mountains, the tundra and the taiga, the ice and the storms, and they stay. The relationships between people and place – the tension and the love, and the shapes that tension and that love can take – are the main focus of this book.

It was more than a decade after that day beside the window, when I dreamed my way around the world, that I finally set out to do it for real. I had spent half of those years away from Shetland. I had been to university, in Scotland and in Copenhagen, then lived and worked in Prague. I had found new directions and pursued them. And then I had come back, through choice, finally, rather than necessity. During those intervening years I thought so often about the parallel, imagining and reimagining the line, that when eventually I decided to follow it, I hardly paused to ask myself why. Now, though, I think I know the reasons.

It was curiosity, first of all. I wanted to explore the parallel, and to see those places to which my own place was tied. I wanted to learn about where I was and what it meant to be there. I wanted to come back laden with that knowledge, and to write it down.

Then there was restlessness – that fizzing pressure within that makes me long for what is elsewhere, for what is far away. That restlessness, that joy and curse that I have known for most of my life, brings unease when I ought to be content; it brings contentment when I ought to be uneasy. It sends me out into the world, almost against my will.

But finally, and perhaps most potently, it was homesickness that made me go. It was a desire to return to somewhere I belonged. My relationship with Shetland had always been fraught and undermined by my own past, and somehow I imagined that by going – by following the parallel around the world – that could change. To make such a journey, in which the final, certain destination must be home, was an act of faithfulness. It was a commitment that, for the first time in my life, I felt ready to make.

And so I went, visiting in turn each country on the sixtieth parallel. I travelled westward, with the sun and with the seasons, to Greenland in spring, North America in summer, Russia in autumn and the Nordic countries in winter. But I began by finding the line.

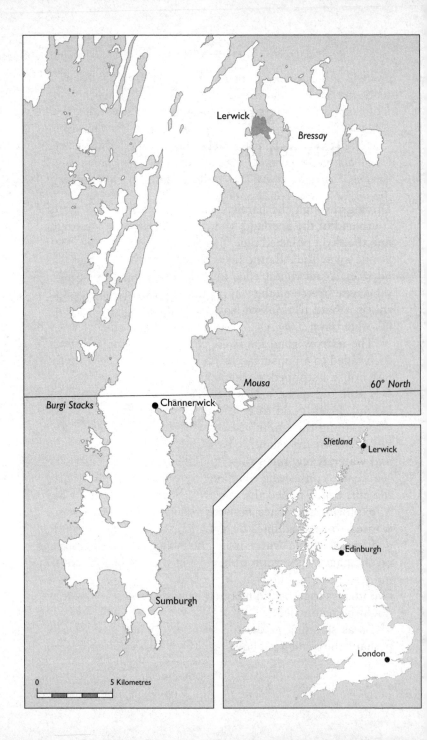

SHETLAND
between the hill and the sea

Driving through the hamlets of Bigton and Ireland at the south end of the Shetland Mainland, the sun was icy bright and the sky a polished blue, barely troubled by clouds. Half a mile away the Atlantic lay like a desert, and beyond, the horizon, a soft, blunt edge interrupting a view that might otherwise stretch all the way around the world. On days like this it is hard to think of leaving. Days like this extinguish all other days.

The narrow road I was on stooped towards the coast, then faded to an unsurfaced track. A mile or so beyond the last house I stopped, parked the car and got out. The air was still and quiet, and warm enough to leave my jacket behind. It felt good to be there, to inhabit the day. Somewhere along this stretch of coast, the sixtieth parallel tied the ocean to the island, passing unmarked between land and water. A few miles or so to the east, it would meet the sea again, connecting Shetland to Norway. As I reached the cliff top, I pulled the map from my bag and unfolded it, exploring the space between where I was and where I wanted to be. The lines on the map were solid and stark, dividing the blue water from the white land. Everything on the page was certain of itself, but the world in front of me was nothing like that. It took a moment to pull these two images together, to merge them, and imagine how they might be reconciled.

I was standing at the top of a steep-sided cove, a *geo*, perhaps thirty metres above the water. From there the land fell sharply towards a bouldered beach, and then the sea, where a thick mat of kelp was tousled by the ebbing tide. Half a dozen seals, alert to my silhouette, abandoned their positions on the rocks and heaved themselves back into the waves. Once safe, they turned to look more carefully at this figure above them, unable to restrain their curiosity. Just offshore, three skerries lay littered with cormorants, black wings outstretched, as the sea around them shivered and shook in the sunlight. Far beyond, to the northwest, the island of Foula lay like a great wave on the horizon. If my map-reading skills were to be trusted, these skerries were the Billia Cletts, which would place me just a few hundred metres south of where I wanted to be. As I walked carefully along the cliff edge the seals were still visible below, their thick bodies dark in the clear water. I stepped slowly, on grey rocks glorious with colour; each stone was splashed yellow-orange by lichen, every crack and crevice was speck-led with sea pinks.

The cliffs along this part of the coast are heavily pitted with caves, hollows and geos. In winter, this side of Shetland meets the full weight of the Atlantic and the southwesterly gales that thunder their way across the ocean. Waves that began life thousands of miles away find their way to these shores, growing larger and more powerful as they go. Water carves itself into the land, and throws giant boulders up the cliffs like marbles. Pondering the many battered coastlines of the world, in her book *The Sea around Us*, Rachel Carson concluded: 'it seems unlikely that any coast is visited more wrathfully by the sea's waves than the Shetlands and the Orkneys'. Summer visitors may imagine these islands to be only a timid north, a place protected from the climatic sever-ities of other northern lands. But bring that visitor back in the middle of a winter storm and they would feel differently. This is one of the windiest places in Europe, and recounting stories of storms past is a favourite occupation for islanders.

There is, for instance, the 'Hogmanay Hurricane' of New Year's Eve, 1991, in which gusts of over 173 miles per hour were recorded before the anemometer was torn from the ground. Then there is the month of January 1993, which brought a record twenty-five days of gales, and saw the oil tanker *Braer* wrecked on the coast, just south of the parallel. Wind is the dominant and most extreme element of Shetland's climate. It can, at times, seem so utterly unremitting that the air itself becomes a physical presence, as solid as a clenched fist. And on those rare calm days its absence can be shocking and wonderful.

It is this violence, of wind and sea, combined with its glacial past, that makes Shetland's coastline what it is: a ragged, fractal form. 'Hardly anything can be imagined,' wrote John Shirreff in 1814, 'more irregular than the shape of this island.' According to the Ordnance Survey, the coastline of Shetland amounts to almost 1,700 miles – sixteen per cent of Scotland's total – and a glance at the map shows why. The largest of the islands, known as 'the Mainland', is fifty miles long, north to south, and just twenty at its widest point. But nowhere is more than three miles from the sea. This southern end is a peninsula, almost thirty miles in length and rarely three wide, which extends like a finger from the fist of the central Mainland. Further north, the coast is a panoply of beaches, coves, steep sea cliffs and narrow inlets, known as *voes*. These voes, like mini-fjords, are deep valleys, flooded by the rising sea after the last ice age. They bite into the land, creating distance, and making the ocean always, everywhere, inescapable.

When Shetland emerged from beneath the ice, 12,000 years ago, it was an empty place. There was no vegetation, no birds, no mammals, no life at all. It was a blank space, waiting to be filled. And as the climate steadily improved, that process of filling began. Lichens, mosses and low shrubs were the first colonisers, followed by sea birds, exploiting the abundant food resources of the North Atlantic. As more birds arrived, they carried with them the seeds of other plants, on their feet and in their stomachs.

The first land mammals in Shetland were people, who arrived around 6,000 years ago. The islands that met these original immigrants would have looked very different from the islands of today. Low woodland dominated – birch, juniper, alder, oak, willow – as well as tall herbs and ferns, particularly around the coast. It was a lush, green and mild place, and the lack of land prey, of deer in particular, was more than compensated for by the lack of predators and of competition. There were none of the wolves and bears the settlers had left behind in Scotland. Here they found an abundance of birds, providing meat and eggs, as well as seals, walrus, whales and fish.

This early settlement of Shetland coincided with the latter stages of a major change in lifestyle in northern Europe. Agriculture, which began in the Fertile Crescent of the Middle East, had gradually spread west and north across the continent as the climate improved and stabilised. Land that had once been scoured and scarred by ice was being transformed by the hands of people. Forests were cut down and burned, and the space given over to domestic animals. The early Shetlanders were also early farmers, and it is hard not to be impressed by their achievements. That they managed to cross the dangerous waters between Britain and the islands in their fragile, skin-covered boats, and in sufficient numbers to build extensive communities, is astonishing enough. But that they also managed to take considerable quantities of livestock with them – pigs, sheep, goats and cattle – is doubly so. These animals, and the people that brought them, were to prove the greatest factor in altering and reshaping the landscape once the ice retreated.

Shetland was at the very far edge of the world for these settlers. Beyond the edge, in fact. It was as far north as it was possible to go through Britain, and the people that came took huge risks. So why did they bother? What pulled them northwards? Could it be that the spirit of adventure was enough – that the cliffs of Shetland, just visible on the horizon from Orkney, taunted people until they could resist no longer? Was it simply human beings exploring the limits of what was possible?

It is tempting to suspect this might be so. But there are other alternatives. There is, in particular, the possibility that the development of agriculture itself may have pushed the settlers onwards. Changes in land use in northern Britain were placing pressure on the available space, and creating tension and conflict between neighbouring peoples. A society without walls or borders was evolving into one in which they were essential. Perhaps it was precisely this tension that drove people north to Shetland.

There was a light breeze now, spilling up and over the cliff top, and fulmars were clinging to it, riding like fairground horses up and down on the shimmering air. One bird lifted higher, close to my head, and hung for a moment against the wind. He seemed almost to float there, and as I watched him I was sure he was looking straight back. For those few seconds we eyed each other, fascinated: me by his sublime disregard for gravity, and he by my clumsy bulk and strange attachment to the earth. Fulmars must be the most inquisitive of seabirds. They seem unable to ignore cliff walkers, pestering them with nosy flybys and showing off their aerobatic skills. They are graceful, but with an air of menace too. Something about them – their blazing, black eyes perhaps, shadowed in front, with a comma flick behind, or their bulbous, petrel beaks – gives them a sinister expression. It is an appearance that is only reinforced by the sharp, clattering cackles of those birds ensconced on their nests, and their habit of throwing up a vile, oily substance on those unfortunate enough to step too close.

Further along the cliff top I reached the Burn of Burgistacks, where wheatears scattered at my approach, each clacking like pebbles in a cloth bag. As I walked they kept their distance ahead of me, hopping a little further with every few steps I took. The burn here clambers hastily towards the sea, down a rocky slope and then a brief waterfall, lined with sopping green moss. Beyond the burn were the Burgi Stacks themselves. And then, according to the map, I was almost at the parallel.

I stopped, and looked carefully at the contours of the land. It was harder than I'd expected it to be to distinguish one point from another, and to be sure exactly where I was. The map showed a cave, over which my line appeared to cross, but from where I stood the cave was entirely hidden. I walked north until I was sure I had crossed the parallel, then retraced my steps. As I peered over the edge of a steep scree slope, the map's clean lines were shattered into stones and grass and waves. The angle of the cliff and the jutting rocks prevented any kind of certainty.

I was tempted then to climb down the slope towards the water, where things might be clearer. There was, it seemed, an almost navigable route down. But it would take me alongside two fat, fluffy fulmar chicks, who would no doubt relish the opportunity to practise their vomiting skills. It was a stupid idea, and I thought better of it. I sat instead on the cool grass, the map open in front of me, tracing the lines with my fingers.

I was hot and thirsty, and annoyed at myself for not bringing a GPS to make things clearer. For a moment it all seemed arbitrary and pointless; there could be no real certainty like this. But still I wanted a fixed point, a starting block from which to begin. So I looked again at the paper, read again every word of the surrounding area: to the south, the Burgi Stacks, the cave, then the Seat of Mandrup and Sheep Pund to the north. Just east was the Green of Mandrup, the field behind me.

And then I saw it. Almost completely hidden by those words – 'Green of Mandrup' – but just protruding from behind the letters on either side, was a solid, straight line: a fence. And as it reached the cliff, it corresponded with the parallel. I stood and faced east, following the posts that ran through the field and up the hill, and then looked back to where the fence ended in a muddle of wire and wood hanging over the cliff edge. So this was it: sixty degrees north of the equator. This was my starting line.

＊

Geography begins at the only point of which we can be certain. It begins inside. And from there, from inside, rises a single question: where am I?

Imagine yourself stood upon a hill. Or better, imagine yourself stood on a tall hill on a small island, the horizon visible in every direction – a perfect, unbroken line. From early morning until late in the night you stand there. You watch the sun rise from one side of the island and arc its way above, moving slowly and predictably through the sky until it reaches the opposite horizon, where it gradually disappears. As the light fades, stars freckle against the mounting darkness. They too turn about you, on an axis rooted at the North Star, Polaris. This great arena of night and day seems to roll over the stationary world and surround you with its movement. And that question rises: where am I?

The universe that we can see is a place of mirrors and illusions, tricks of the eye and the mind, and it takes a great leap of scientific faith to come to terms with the facts as we now know them to be: that nothing is still; that both our universe and our planet are in ceaseless motion. To look upwards and to acknowledge this is to take a nauseating lurch of the imagination. It is to be overwhelmed not just by a feeling of insignificance, but of fear, vulnerability and exhilaration. Amid all this movement, this unfathomable distance, it seems somehow impossible that we could be anywhere at all.

But our understanding of where we are on the Earth has not been built with this celestial motion in mind. Since people first began to use the sun and stars as navigational aids, they have done so by being ignorant of, or by ignoring such disorientating facts. That the North Star is not a stable point within the universe does not matter so long as it seems to be a stable point. That the sun does not turn around the Earth makes no difference if it continues to appear to do so, and that its appearance is predictable. For the roots of that question – where am I? – are not so much philosophical, nor exactly scientific; they are practical. Where we are only truly makes sense in so far as it relates to where we have been and where we want to be. In order to move in a purposeful way, to avoid wasting our time and endangering our lives, we must build an image of our location, and where we stand in our surroundings. We must make maps.

I stared out at the calm ocean, at the tide lines laced like skeins of white hair. I looked towards the horizon – blue fastened to blue – and beyond, towards unseen places: to Greenland, to North America, to Russia, Finland, Scandinavia and back here again across the North Sea. I looked out for several minutes, then felt ready to go. I turned and walked up the hill, alongside the fence. From my starting line at the cliff I made my way back along the parallel, glad to be moving again.

Soon, the lavish green that had fringed the shore gave way to low heather and dark, peaty ground. The land flattened into a plateau of purple and olive, trenched and terraced where the turf had been cut. White tufts of bog cotton lay strewn about the hill. Shallow pools of black water crouched below the banks of peat and in the narrow channels that lolled between. I hopped from island to island of solid ground, trying to keep my feet dry, as a skylark hung frantically above, held aloft by the lightness of his song.

After only ten minutes or so I was walking downhill again, into the lush valley that folds around the loch of Vat-setter and the Burn of Maywick, flanked by bright yellow irises. The thick heather faded back into a lighter, leaner green, and on the opposite slope was a field, striped by cut silage. A gust of golden plovers sprang suddenly from the ground ahead, and curled its way over the valley. Two lap-wings crossed their path above the loch, guttering towards the sea with a clumsy kind of grace. I watched the birds until they tumbled out of view, and then continued to the burn below.

The steep descent into the valley meant an equally steep climb out again, on a gravel track that, according to the map, crossed back and forth over the parallel several times before waning into nothing. I carried on, and was soon back amid the peat. The hill rose sharply to 200 metres, and I was hot from the walking, but it was worth it. As I reached the higher ground, the air opened up without warning, and I could see from one side of Shetland to the other: the Atlantic behind and the North Sea in front. Above, wisps of cirrus cloud were combed across a bold sky, as wide as any sky I had ever seen before.

Human beings have always moved from here to there, from one place to another, with a combination of memory, acquired knowledge and curiosity. We have made use, most commonly, of internal maps – remembered routes from one point of significance to another: a place of food, a place of shelter, a place of danger. Elements of these maps would have been passed from generation to generation, in songs and in stories. They were embellished, updated and, if necessary, discarded. These are living maps, where space and direction are sealed off and separated from the world outside. They can be as intricate and mysterious as the songlines of the

Australian Aborigines, or as straightforward as remembering how to reach the shop from your front door.

To build a more concrete image of where we are it has been necessary to externalise our maps: to make pictures of the world. The very first visual maps were of the stars, such as those on the walls of the Lascaux caves in France, drawn more than 16,000 years ago. But looking up at the sky is easy. To draw a picture that could encompass a particular space on the Earth, or encompass the whole planet even, is a far greater challenge. The mapmaker is forced to become other than himself, to imagine the view of the birds. The mapmaker must look down from above and become god-like, re-creating his own world.

Unlike internal or 'story' maps, early world maps were intended as scientific or philosophical exercises rather than navigational guides. Their practicality was limited by two significant factors. Firstly, the ancient Greeks who pioneered cartography had limited geographical knowledge. Centred on the Mediterranean, their maps extended eastward only as far as India, with their westward edge at the Strait of Gibraltar. Beyond these boundaries the world was more or less unknown, though speculation about the grotesque barbarians dwelling in northern Europe and Africa was widespread. The other major problem for the Greek mapmakers was their lack of a practical means of representing distance and shape accurately. What was required to do this was some kind of scale or grid, which could be applied both to the spherical surface of the Earth and, potentially, to a globe or a flat map. That grid was provided in the second century BC, when Hipparchus of Nicaea devised the system that we still use today: measuring the Earth in degrees of arc. Although similar methods had been proposed previously by the Babylonians, Hipparchus' achievement was to divide a circle into 360 degrees of arc, and so provide the foundation stone for trigonometry.

A degree was a measurement of the angle at the centre of a circle, between one radius and another, like the hands on a clock. If the time is three o'clock, the angle between the two hands is 90°: one quarter of a full circle. On the outside of the circle, the points where the two radii, or hands, touch the edge can also be said to be 90° apart. This measurement could further be applied to spheres, like the Earth, with the north-south angle denoted by one measurement – latitude – and the east-west angle by another – longitude. It was then possible, at least theoretically, to give co-ordinates for any place on the planet, and that information could further be used to represent geographical space accurately on a map. This was a revolutionary step for navigation and for cartography.

Whereas longitudinal lines, or meridians, are of equal length, running through both poles, and dividing the planet like the segments of an orange, circles of latitude are parallel lines, progressively decreasing in size, from the planet's full circumference at the equator to a single point at the Poles. They are represented as an angle up to 90° north or south of the equator. At 60° north, where I was standing, the parallel was half the length of the equator, and two thirds of the way to the Pole.

For the Greeks, the pinnacle of their cartographic tradition came in the mid-second century AD, in Roman Alexandria. It was here that Claudius Ptolemy created his *Geographia*, a work that gathered together the geographical knowledge of both the Greeks and the Romans. Ptolemy gave co-ordinates for around 8,000 places, stretching between his Prime Meridian at the Fortunate Isles (Cape Verde) in the west, China in the east, central Africa in the south and Shetland, which he called Thule, in the north. This was the known world, reaching 180 degrees in longitude and eighty in latitude, and Shetland then was at its very edge. Despite all but disappearing for more than 1,000 years, the influence of this book, eventually, was immense.

Today, we need only consult a map to learn of our location, or just press a button on our handheld GPS or phone, which can tell us our longitude and latitude in degrees, minutes and seconds of arc. But still somehow that question feels unanswered, still it gnaws at our certainty. Where am I?

✳

This is a strange place up here, this landscape of peat and heather. Often called generically 'the hill', it forms the core of Shetland, covering more than fifty per cent of the land. From that spot I could have walked to the north of the Mainland, forty miles away, and hardly stepped off it at all. It is a place separate from the places of people, a semi-wild moorland, divided by fence and dyke from the croft land below. It has also been, and in many parts of Shetland remains, a shared place – a common ground – with grazing and peat-cutting rights held collectively by crofters in adjacent communities.

In descriptions of the hill by travellers, certain words recur frequently: barren, desolate, featureless. The land is considered to be missing something, lacking in both aesthetic appeal and agricultural worth. The *Encyclopaedia Britannica* of 1911 proclaimed Shetland's interior to be 'bleak and dreary, consisting of treeless and barren tracts of peat and boulders'. It is a heaving, undulating terrain, without the drama of a mountainscape or the quietude of a valley. It is a place neither tame enough nor wild enough to be considered valuable. It is, in many senses, an in-between land. On the map, there is little to see here but contour lines, and the serpentine scrawl of the burns, where black water chuckles seaward from the inertia of the bog. Looking around, the eye seeks places on which to settle, to focus, but nothing breaks the heavy swell of the land. The hill presents an expanse of sameness that draws the walker in and creates a sense of separation from the world below. There is a kind of space, a vastness, which is somehow surprising in such a limited land. The peatscape opens out and unfolds in what Robert Macfarlane calls 'active expansiveness'. The horizon, the cupola of the sky and the clarity of the air, all become part of the land's measure and its bulk. Together in this arena they uphold an illusion of distance, and make Shetland seem a larger place, a place in which it is possible to become lost. Here you can feel yourself entirely remote from other people, and sit alone, amid an unfamiliar quiet.

Like those who dwell in the shadow of mountains, Shetlanders live with the constant presence of the moor and the hill. It is a presence that is, I think, as central to the character of the islanders as it is to the islands. For just as we inhabit the landscape, the landscape inhabits us, in thought, in myth and in memory; and somehow the openness of the land invites us to become attached, or else attaches itself to us. Our understanding of space and our relationship to that space are affected, and so too is our understanding of time.

We are used to imagining time as a fixed dimension, through which we are moved, steadily and unfalteringly. But there are places where this image seems inadequate, where time itself seems to move at another pace altogether. There are places where we sense the moments rush by, unhindered, so close and so quick that we feel the breath of them as they pass. And then there are other places, such as here on the hill, where time seems to gather itself, to coil and unravel simultaneously. Here the past is closer. We find its memory embedded within the earth, like the eerily preserved bodies, centuries old, drawn out of peat bogs across Europe, with clothes, skin and hair intact. Or like the peat itself, a biological journal of the islands' history. Things move slowly here. Change is stubbornly, solemnly recorded. To examine the land closely, and to take into account its own life and the lives upon and within it, is to be faced with a multitude of other times and other worlds. Here on the hill, where land and sky open out, past and present do the opposite; they wrap themselves tightly together. There is, here, a native timelessness.

It is hardly surprising therefore that the hill has played such a significant role in the mythology of these islands. In particular, it has long been, and remains, the home of Shetland's resident 'hillfolk', the   . Nocturnal, troll-like creatures, sometimes benign and sometimes taking the role of trickster, the best known trow stories tell of musicians, bribed or lured down into the earth beneath the heather. There they must perform in a world where the human measurement of time no longer applies. The fiddle player will entertain his hosts for the evening, and be offered food and drink, even a place to sleep; but he may emerge from his night's performance to find that his children are grown, his wife remarried or long dead. One unfortunate fiddler, Sigurd o' Gord, lost an entire century beneath the hill. He returned home with a tune he had learned, 'Da Trows' Spring', but discovered that everything had changed in his absence: his home belonged to someone else; his family were long gone.

The popularity of these tales refuses to fade. The stories are endlessly repeated, recorded and published, overshadowing virtually all other native folklore, and I'm sure there are still some Shetlanders who claim to have met one of these creatures while out wandering on the hill. The trow may appear suddenly out of the mist, or from behind a rock, or it may even emerge from the rock itself. They are integral, it seems, to the landscape in which they live, and their stubborn persistence, as a subject and as a species, must at least in part be down to the equally stubborn persistence of this, their habitat. It should also be seen, I think, as a manifestation of the ongoing ambivalence in our relationship with that habitat, an ambivalence expressed most clearly in the debates that have raged for years over the building of windfarms in the central Mainland.

The uneasiness that the peatscapes can invoke has deep cultural roots. Human society in Shetland developed together with, rather than simply alongside, the hill, and that development is reflected in the relationship between them. When people first arrived in the islands, peat had not yet begun to form over large areas. It existed in isolated, poorly-drained patches, but the blanket bog that now stretches across much of the land would simply not have been there. The arrival of humans in Shetland, though, coincided with a downturn in the climate. Temperatures dropped and rainfall increased, and in waterlogged, acidic ground, where vegetable matter cannot properly decompose, it instead begins to accumulate as peat. The process would have been a natural one, determined by both soil and climate, but sustained deforestation and agricultural development also played an important role. Further climatic deterioration speeded up the peat growth, and spread the bog across new areas. More and more, Shetlanders were forced to abandon previously useful land that had become saturated, acidic and infertile, and were squeezed into a thin, habitable wedge between the hill and the sea. By 2,000 years ago, the land would have looked much as it does today.

Paradoxically though, the development of peat was eventually to provide the means by which people could survive this climatic shift. For while the destruction of the native woodlands must have contributed to the growth of the bogs, the forest had never been very substantial anyway. The fuel that was available to people, both from indigenous trees and from driftwood, was most likely becoming scarce by the time that peat had grown to useful depths. And it is peat – cut, dried and burned – that has sustained people in these islands ever since. Those communities without access to it struggled, and sometimes failed to survive. It was, until very recently, an essential element of life in Shetland.

Today, electricity, gas, coal and oil have largely replaced peat in island homes. But it is still dug by some, out of habit or nostalgia, or because the smell of burning turf has a warmth and a redolence that cannot be replicated by any other fuel. Its thick, blue-grey smoke is inviting and evocative, wrapping a house in warmth and in memories of warmth. But its necessity has now passed, and there on the hilltop it seems the life of the peat itself may be passing too. On the slopes around me, much of it had eroded to the bedrock, drying out and degrading. And below, as I began descending again, towards Channerwick, I could see great swathes of black and grey all around, scars of soil and of stone. In the autumn of 2003, after two dry summers and one dry winter, a single night of heavy rain resulted in thousands of tonnes of peat slipping off the hill where I stood, covering the road, destroying a bridge and walls, killing sheep. Other landslides have occurred elsewhere in the islands since, and as the climate continues to change – with temperatures rising and both droughts and storms increasing – the illusion of stability and permanence that exists on the hill is likely to be shattered more and more often.

I paused just above the main road, where a small, yellow sign confirmed the latitude. Ahead of me were Hoswick and Sandwick, hidden behind the crest of the next hill; and beyond them lay the sea, and the island of Mousa. There is no cover here, no shelter or protection. Everything is exposed like the bare rock scars. A kind of melancholy had settled on me as I crossed the moor, but I was reluctant to move on and leave the hill behind. I sat on the heather gazing at the sky above, where a few, sluggish clouds drifted east towards the sea. Then I lay back and closed my eyes for a moment, and dreamed I was exactly where I was.

*

I first visited Shetland when I was about five years old, on a holiday with my parents. My mother's elder brother had moved to the islands from Belfast in the late 1960s for work, then married a Shetlander and had a family. My other uncle had followed and stayed, and we came to visit them several times. My mother and father had considered moving north before I was born. Both of them felt drawn here, away from the south of England where I spent my first few years, but it was not until after they separated that my mother eventually made the move. My memories of those early trips are vague, and have mingled with photographs from the family album, which fix them more solidly but less certainly in place. They are images more than they are true memories, snapshot moments that carry little weight. A boy on a beach, playing and swimming in the sunshine; games and tears in the Lerwick street where my uncle lived.

When we moved north permanently, my mother, brother and I, I was ten years old. My parents had separated some time before that, but family life in Sussex had otherwise continued much as I had always known it. I was too young to really understand the significance of their split, and was anyway surrounded, always, by love.

The idea of a relocation felt like an adventure, as such things always do to a child. From the moment it was first discussed, I was excited and eager to go. The reality though was different, like going away on holiday and discovering, while there, that you can never go back home. That half my family were with me did not detract from the sense that I had been lifted up and dropped in an alien place, a place that was not and could not be my home. The word for it, I suppose, is deracination – to be uprooted. That was how it seemed to me. My past was elsewhere, my childhood was elsewhere, my friends, my grandparents, my father were elsewhere.

That feeling of division and separation cut deep into me then. A sense that who I was and what I needed were not here but somewhere else grew inside me, and continued to grow. That sense evolved, over time, into the restlessness that dogs me even today and that triggered, in part, this journey. It evolved too into an unshakable feeling of exile and of homesickness, and a corresponding urge to extinguish that feeling: to be connected, to belong, to be a part of somewhere and no longer apart. It was what Scott Russell Sanders has called 'The longing to become an inhabitant', intensified and distorted by an unwillingness to inhabit the place in which I had to live.

My separation from Shetland was, I thought, as obvious to others as it was to me. And my antipathy, I believed, was reciprocated. According to the twin pillars of island identity – accent and ancestry – I was an outsider and would always be so. Growing up in Lerwick I imagined myself unable ever to truly fit in. I was often unhappy in school, sometimes bullied, and it was those differences, naturally, on which bullies would focus. For the first time I discovered that I was English, not because I had chosen to be so, but because that was the label that was tied around my neck. For a while I wore it proudly, like a badge of distinction, but in the end it didn't seem to fit. My unsettledness in those early years, my sense of exile and longing, did not find a positive direction until I was sixteen, when I decided to go and study music and to live with my father. To make that choice – to decide the place where I would be – was enormously important. And then came the accident, and choice, again, was gone.

*

Shetland, like other remote parts of Scotland, is scarred by the remnants of the past, by history made solid in the landscape. Rocks, reordered and rearranged, carry shadows of the people that moved them. They are the islands' memory. From the ancient field dykes and boundary lines, burnt mounds and forts, to the crumbling croft houses, abandoned by the thousands who emigrated at the end of the nineteenth century, the land is witness to every change, but it is loss that it remembers most clearly. For some, these rocks reek of mortality. Their forms are an oppressive reminder that we, too, will leave little behind us. In 'The Broch of Mousa', the poet Vagaland wrote of how 'in the islands darkness falls / On homes deserted, and on ruined walls; / The tide of life recedes.' People have come and gone from these islands, and with them have passed 'their ways, their thoughts, their songs; / To earth they have returned.' We are left only with the memory of stones.

The island of Mousa was once a place of people. It was once home to families, to fishermen and farmers, who lived and died there. But now the people are gone and their homes deserted. The island has been left to the sheep, the birds and the seals, and, in the summer at least, to the tourists. On the day I visited, there were fifteen of us – British, Scandinavian and North American – making the journey on the little ferry, *Solan IV*, which carries passengers between April and September. It is a short trip from the stone pier in Sandwick to the jetty on the island, and as we galloped across the grey sound I looked about at the other passengers. One, a man wearing beige combat trousers, checked shirt and red baseball cap, consulted a handheld GPS for the full five minutes of the crossing. He never looked up, never looked out at the water or the approaching island, just stared at the little screen in front of him. It was an odd way to experience the journey, but I was jealous of his gadget, and of the accuracy it promised. I wanted to see what he could see.

A remote island of just one and a half square miles might seem an unusual tourist attraction, but people come to Mousa for several reasons. First, there is the opportunity to explore an island once occupied, now uninhabited (what you might call the St Kilda factor). There is, too, the chance to see birds and seals, which take advantage of the lack of people to breed here in large numbers. But most of all, people come here for the broch. While Mousa is just one of around one hundred known Iron Age broch sites in Shetland, and several hundred in the whole of Scotland, it is nevertheless unique, for only this one still looks much as it did when it was first built, over 2,000 years ago. For this fact alone Mousa would be impressive, having withstood two millennia of human and climatic violence; but no less remarkable than its longevity is the actual structure itself, standing at forty-four feet: the tallest prehistoric building in Britain. In shape, it is rather like a power station cooling tower, bulging slightly at the base, where its diameter is fifty feet, and slimming gently, then straightening to vertical towards the top. Constructed entirely of flat stones, the broch is held together by nothing more than the weight of the stones above and the skill of the original builders. It is an outstanding architectural achievement. Inside is a courtyard, separated from the world by double walls more than three metres thick. And between the two outer walls a stairway winds upwards, giving access to cells at various levels, and ultimately to the top of the tower, where visitors can look at the island spread out around them.

Will Self has called Mousa Broch 'one of my sacred sites. For me, comparable to the pyramids'. And that comparison is understandable. The broch is beautiful and mysterious, imposing and tantalisingly intact. Yet we know almost nothing of the people who – around the same time that Ptolemy was marking Shetland on the map – decided to build this structure. It is safe to assume that the architects of Scotland's brochs were a militarised people, for the towers' defensive capabilities are obvious. But there is something about this broch that implies more than simply defence. Its massive size seems beyond necessity, and the sheer extravagance of it suggests that, if security was the primary concern, it must have been built in a state of extreme paranoia. So perhaps a more likely possibility is that the brochs were built not for defence alone, but as acts of self-glorification by Iron Age chieftains. They were status symbols, born of a bravado much like that which created skyscrapers in the twentieth century: a combination of functionality and showing off.

That this particular example has survived so perfectly for so long is partly a result of its remoteness, and partly because nobody has ever had the need to take it to pieces. While other ancient buildings have been plundered for useful material over the millennia, Mousa's beaches are still crowded with perfect, flat stones, providing all the material the island's inhabitants ever required. The rocks which helped to create such an extraordinary structure have remained plentiful enough to help ensure its long life. And today, those rocks are protecting other lives too. Press your ear to the walls of the broch and you will hear the soft churring and grunting of storm petrels, the tiny seabirds that patter their way above the waves by day, returning to the safety of their nests at night. Seven thousand storm petrels – eight percent of Britain's population – nest on this island, on the beaches and in the broch itself. The building seems almost to breathe with the countless lives concealed within: past and present hidden, sheltered among the rocks.

The people who built this broch, who lived in and around it, seem far out of reach to us today, an enigma. Archaeologists and historians examine the available clues carefully and they make assessments, suppositions. But in our desire to eradicate mystery from the past, and to understand and know these people, we forget one crucial point. We miss the real mystery. Sitting on the grass beneath the broch, looking back towards the Mainland, I scratched my wrists and brushed the midges from my face. There was no wind, and the insects were taking advantage of the opportunity to feed. The clouds hung low over the sound, and draped softly onto the hills across the water. What struck me then, as I leaned back against the ancient stone wall, was not the great distance and difference that lay between now and then, nor was it the tragedy of all we do not know. What struck me was the sense of continuity, and the deep determination of people to live in this place.

Rebecca West once wrote that certain places 'imprint the same stamp on whatever inhabitants history brings them, even if conquest spills out one population and pours in another wholly different in race and philosophy'. This stamp is what Lawrence Durrell called 'the invisible constant'; it is the thread that holds the history of a place together, the sense of sameness that cuts through the past like a furrow through a field.

In Shetland, human society has evolved in both gradual and sudden movements. For a few hundred years people built brochs, and then they stopped. In the two millennia that followed many other changes took place. New people came, bringing a new language and a new religion, before they too disappeared when the Vikings arrived in the late eighth century. Yet despite these changes, despite all that came and went in that time, always it was the land that dictated the means of survival. The Norsemen arrived as Vikings, but they became Shetlanders. They became fishermen and farmers, just as the Picts had been, just as the broch-builders had been, and all those before them. Crops were sown and harvested; sheep and cattle were reared and killed. The land scarred the people, just as the people, in turn, scarred the land. If there is an 'invisible constant' or identity bestowed by a place upon its inhabitants, it could only be found there, in that relationship, that engagement with the land. It is not inherited, but earned.

As I walked slowly back towards the boat, a cloud of Arctic terns – called *tirricks* in Shetland – billowed like a smoke signal from a beach just ahead. Some of the birds drifted southwards, swooping then hovering above me, pinned like little crucifixes against the sky. Everything about the terns is sharp – beak, wings, tail – even their cries are serrated. And their tiny forms belie an aggression that can terrify the unwary walker. Like the Arctic and great skuas that share this island with them, tirricks attack without hesitation anyone who seems to threaten their nesting ground. There is no subtlety in their assault. They simply wheel and swarm above, then dive, each in turn, screaming as they drop. It is enough to discourage all but the most determined of trespassers.

It occurred to me, almost too late, that I had forgotten why I was here on the island. The departure time for the ferry was approaching, but I pulled the map out of my bag and tried to locate the parallel on the paper. I was only a hundred metres or so from the line, it seemed, so I hurried ahead to find it. But when I turned the next corner I stopped again, for standing just where I was heading was the man in the red baseball cap, staring down at his GPS. Clearly he too was looking for the parallel. The man took a few steps back, and consulted the gadget again, head down. By this time he was only ten metres or so away, and soon noticed that I was standing watching. He turned, as if to ask what I was doing. I smiled the best smile I could muster, which probably looked more half-witted than friendly. He didn't smile back. I wasn't sure what to do. I could have spoken to him, told him that we were both looking for the same thing, but somehow the seconds passed and we continued to stand there, each hoping the other would just go away. I had no particular desire to explain myself, and he, it seemed, felt the same way. It was an awkward moment, and in the end it was me who gave up and moved on. I nodded, then put my head down and walked towards the jetty, where the little boat was waiting.

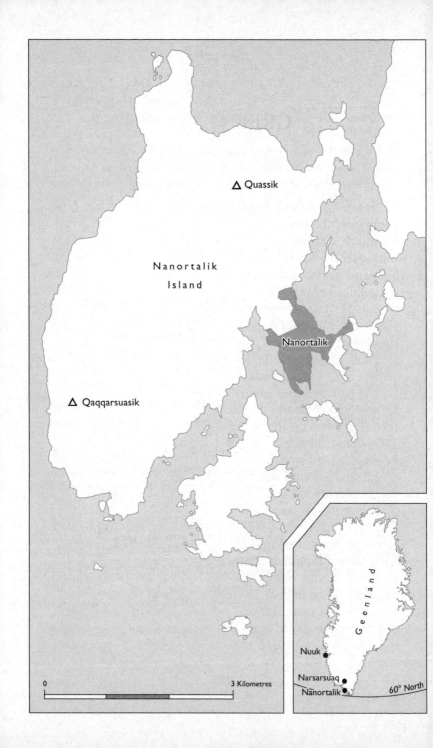

GREENLAND
in passing

To reach Greenland from Shetland required a detour in completely the wrong direction, through Scotland and then Denmark, via Amsterdam. From Copenhagen I took a flight back over the North Atlantic, crossing almost directly above Shetland again, and arrived in Narsarsuaq, a tiny airport that clings between Greenland's southwestern coast and its icecap. My final destination was Nanortalik, a village further south still, but I took my time in getting there, enjoying the chance to explore a place I expected never to see again.

Public transport in Greenland is by boat or by helicopter – there are no roads between communities – and in springtime it is largely the latter. On the last of my flights, from Qaqortoq to Nanortalik, we lifted calmly from the tarmac, then thundered up and over the fjord, flying low above bare valleys and hillsides, over tundra, lakes, rocks and snow. Below, the land stretched out in a patchwork of brown and green, studded with scraps of white and blue and grey. And then, suddenly, the sea.

In my travels south along the coast I had seen a lot of ice. In Narsaq, I had walked across beaches strewn with stranded bergs, decomposing in the warm spring sunshine. They were a thousand forms: some pointed, with sharp fingers and shards; others smooth, like the curves of muscle and flesh on an animal. Some were as large as cars or caravans, others I could lift and hold in the palm of my hand: tiny fragments, faded almost to nothing. I wandered among these shapes, watching their quiet disappearance, and I felt a peculiar kind of grief. Here was a difficult presence, almost alive and almost unreal, like shadows made solid, or crystalline astonishment. Out in the water beyond, the icebergs were much bigger, but still somehow precarious. They seemed out of place in the sunshine, beside the colour of the town and beneath the blackness of the mountains. Bright, blue-white against the vitreous shiver of the water, the ice like clouds took form in the imagination. Reclining bathers, ships, mushrooms, whales and kayakers. They seemed caught in constant imbalance, between two worlds.

But now, from the window of the Air Greenland helicopter, I saw something else entirely. Stretched out beneath us, reaching away to the horizon and beyond, was an immense carpet of sea ice, a dense mosaic of flat, white plates like crazy-paving on the dark water. I felt immersed. As far as I could see, the fractured ice lay tightly packed. Great slabs the size of tennis courts, and bigger, were crammed together, and between them smaller pieces in every possible shape. This was *storis* – pack ice formed in the Arctic Ocean, east of Greenland. Each winter, a dense band of this ice drifts southwards on the East Greenland current, rounding Cape Farewell in the first months of the year, then moving slowly up the southwest coast, disintegrating as it goes. The whole scene was unfathomable. There was nothing for the eye to hold on to; all sense of scale was lost. Here and there an iceberg protruded, but it was impossible to know how large they were. When we buzzed low over a cargo ship, slogging its way through the solid ocean, it looked far too small, like a toy, dwarfed by the cracked expanse of white and glacial blue all around it. I took the camera from my bag and held it up to the window.

That picture hangs above my desk as I write. A blanket of shattered ice leads out to the horizon, swollen by a blue-black bruise reflecting the clear water beyond. I return to the image over and over, as if searching for something that I know is there but cannot seem to focus upon. Framed within that photograph is the very thing I came to Greenland to see. It is an image of the north: bright and brittle, terrifying and intensely beautiful. Looking back on it now, the distance between myself and that ice-laden image stretches out and becomes an unimaginable gulf. I have tried to forge a connection, a bridge between, but the picture remains shocking, long after I hung it there.

The helicopter came to rest on the rough landing strip at Nanortalik, the southernmost of Greenland's main settlements. The village is decked out in northern Scandinavian uniform, its wooden houses red, yellow, purple, green, even pink – some pastel pale, others vivid as children's paint. The village is home to around 1,300 people, with a few smaller hamlets scattered through the surrounding fjords. It sits on one of the many islands that pepper this coast, but is no more isolated for that. The hostel where I was to stay was at the other side of town from the heliport, beyond the houses and the main street, at the old harbour with its white wooden church and timber cottages. Most of the buildings around the harbour were occupied by the town museum, but one little red bungalow served as a hostel, in which I was the only guest.

I threw my bag into the living room, where two bunk beds huddled around a gas fire, and went back outside to sit on the front step. The morning had cleared and warmed a little, though there was a bitter breeze lifting off the sea. The bay in front of the hostel was loosely cluttered with ice, just clear enough for boats to make their way in and out of the harbour. There was a slow shifting of everything, almost discernible as I sat watching, and now and then a booming crack and splash as an iceberg split and collapsed into the water. The view from the doorway was southwestward, out to sea, but took in the hunched bulk of Qaqqarsuasik, the island's highest point. From the step I could see ravens swoop and wheel around the dark slopes, silhouetted as they rose above the peak, then almost hidden against the blackness of the rock. Their caws, clicks and splutters echoed around the bay, puncturing the silence as they punctured the air with their flight. A flurry of sounds – manic gulps and underwater barks – rained down on me as I sat, listening, watching, until hunger persuaded me to move.

*

Shaped like a great arrowhead hurled southward from the Pole, Greenland is the largest island in the world, stretching from Cape Morris Jessup, 83° north of the equator, to Cape Farewell, just south of 60°. From its earliest, uncertain appearances on the map, it has largely been a blank space, an enormous emptiness into which centuries of European fears, myths and misconceptions have been poured. This is a land of concentrated northness, where childhood images of Eskimos and polar bears, ice and isolation, come together. It is a paradoxical place, both intensely alien and deeply familiar. Geographically and culturally it is a meeting point between Europe and the American Arctic, where north and south come awkwardly together. Here, certain tensions and certain conflicts between these two worlds are played out, day to day.

But this situation is far from new, for it is here that European people first encountered American people more than 1,000 years ago, and it is here that two visions of the Arctic and two very different understandings of place have been tried and savagely tested. The familiar story of Greenland is the European story: the westward advance of the Norsemen at the end of the first millennium AD. With their empire expanding, from Shetland and Orkney south to Britain, Ireland and beyond, and from Faroe north into Iceland, the Vikings were apparently unstoppable. They flourished in these northern lands – lands once considered beyond the habitable edge of the world – and it was not long before they ventured further still, into places that no European had ever gone before.

But in some ways this story is unlike other colonial histories. For one thing, there is the rather peculiar fact that, in Greenland, the colonisers arrived before the colonised; the Norse reached this island prior to the arrival of the Inuit. When Eirik the Red first landed in Greenland in 982AD, somewhere not far from present day Nanortalik, Greenland was populated by an entirely different people, the Dorset – part of a wider northern culture, known as the Tuniit, which is now extinct – but their small population was restricted to the far northwestern coast. This might have come as a surprise to Eirik, had he known, for although the Icelander met no-one as he explored the western fjords, he did find evidence of people. It was clear that he was not the first man to reach this place. Old settlements were still visible, the remains of hearths and homes still apparent. But no fires had been lit along this coast for more than 1,000 years. The people that had been here – the Saqqaq, from 2400 BC, and the early-Dorset, from 900 BC – had long since died out or retreated northwards.

By calling this place Greenland – 'for he said that people would be much more tempted to go there if it had an attractive name', as the *Grænlendinga Saga* has it – Eirik the Red succeeded in convincing enough of his fellow Icelanders to follow him to the new land to found two major settlements. The larger of these, known as the Eastern Settlement, was based on this southwestern coast; the other was further north, where Nuuk, Greenland's capital, now lies.

Initially, the Norse lived much as they had in Iceland and elsewhere, as farmers. Their options were limited somewhat by the shortage of suitable ground for crops, but the climate was good and the colony succeeded, with large numbers of goats, sheep and cattle reared at the wealthiest farms in the south. The Norse hunted too, making use of the plentiful seals to supplement their diet. Soon, a trade in northern goods – walrus ivory, furs, polar bears, and narwhal or 'unicorn' horns – opened up between Greenland and Bergen in Norway. This was a valuable trade. Ivory and furs were luxury items in the south, and narwhals' tusks could fetch more than their weight in gold. King Christian V of Denmark would later have an entire throne constructed from these horns, and Queen Elizabeth I of England could have had a new castle built for the price she paid for a single, decorated tooth. But the Norse probably saw very little of this money; coins would not have helped them much in Greenland. They exchanged their Arctic treasure for iron, timber and other necessary materials. And just as importantly, this market allowed them to keep open the contact between the colony and Europe, to remain part of the Scandinavian, Christian world. They had neither the knowledge nor the desire to survive without this ongoing connection.

As exploration of the area expanded, the settlers began to encounter other peoples, whom they called *skraelings*: wretches. Despite the all-encompassing word, there were at least three distinct groups that came into contact with the Norse. The first of these were late-Dorset Tuniit, whom the settlers would have met as they travelled north on hunting trips. The second were Algonquin Indians living on the east coast of North America, whose violent resistance, probably more than any other factor, put an end to the Vikings' western expansion. The final group encountered by the Norse were the Thule, ancestors of today's Inuit, who first arrived in the country between 1200 and 1300 AD, when the colonies were at their strongest. A highly adaptable and successful marine culture, the Thule emerged first in the Bering Strait region of what is now Alaska. In addition to hunting and fishing they had also learned to use dog sleds and to build boats and kayaks, from which they caught whales, using harpoons made of iron. During the Mediaeval Warm Period, when the Norse were pushing westward across the North Atlantic, the Thule made a similar push eastward through the Arctic. They understood how to live in this environment; they were deeply at home in the landscape. But they too were traders, and the supply of iron for making tools was critical to their success. In Alaska this iron was most likely acquired through exchange with peoples in East Asia, but there were rich sources of iron in the east too, at meteor crash sites in northern Greenland, and in the hands of the Norse settlers.

Recent archaeological evidence suggests that the migration of the Thule across the Arctic may not have come about merely through nomadic curiosity or as part of a natural expansion of their homeland, but because the existence of iron – and of the Norse themselves – had become known to them. Indeed, far from being an insular and isolated society, as they were long portrayed, the Inuit's development as a culture may effectively have been defined by their contact with other peoples, from both west and east.

When the Norse finally met the Thule, in the thirteenth or fourteenth century, an uneasy balance was struck between the two cultures. Most likely neither trusted the other very much, and for understandable reasons. Throughout their time in Greenland the Norse proved themselves to be exceedingly poor when it came to public relations. Their default approach on encountering unknown people was violence, and no doubt tensions simmered in all of their dealings with these new neighbours. Ultimately though, it was not hostility or mistrust that was to upset the balance between these two peoples. It was something far more mundane, and with unexpectedly dramatic consequences. It was the weather.

In the centuries of Viking exploration and Norse settlement, the north had been enjoying a mild climate and hospitable summers. Temperatures had peaked around the time Eirik first arrived in Greenland, when, according to *Njal's Saga*, corn was being grown on Icelandic farms. But this fruitfulness was not to last. From the late fourteenth century onwards, there was a significant cooling of the climate in Europe and the Arctic. Winters became longer and more severe, and summers less predictable. It was a trend that was to continue. Farming in Greenland was immediately made more difficult. Crops failed, meaning fewer animals could be kept, and the Norse soon found themselves in trouble. Seal hunting may have increased to cover some of the loss in reared meat, but it seems the farmers were slow to adapt. They held on to their way of life even as it became impossible, as though familiarity itself could offer them some kind of protection.

There were other consequences of this colder weather, too. Sea ice increased, so that trading ships from Norway, already intermittent after the arrival of the Black Death in Europe and the rise of the Hanseatic League, now ceased entirely. This was a serious blow, both materially and psychologically. The Norse found themselves isolated from Europe, and all trading relations with the Thule came suddenly, necessarily, to an end. This would not have gone down well. A good supply of iron was as important to the hunters as it was to the farmers, and it is likely that, unable to obtain it through trade, they began to take it by force.

Many theories have emerged over the years to account for the ultimate failure of the Norse colonies in Greenland. Plagues, inbreeding, attacks by pirates: all have been blamed. Jared Diamond has argued that overuse of the land and a taboo against eating fish could have been the deciding factors. But perhaps no final nail is required in this particular coffin, for the facts themselves are enough to lead to the conclusion. The climate changed; farming became increasingly difficult and certainly impossible in places; trade with Norway and with the Thule ceased; relations between the groups soured, and conflicts erupted over scarce resources. The threat of starvation would then have hung over the colonies like a vulture. Some people may have tried to flee eastwards to Iceland, others may even have fled west. Those who remained died. In 1350, the Western Settlement was found to be empty of people, their few remaining animals roaming free. And before the end of the fifteenth century, all of the Norse were gone. While the Inuit had continued to thrive, and had expanded their range across the American North, the Europeans had been entirely wiped out. For the proud, hardy Scandinavians, it was a terrible conclusion. The creeping cold, the suffocating fear, the inevitable end: this was a slow Arctic nightmare that would recur many times in years to come. For another century, or perhaps even less, the Inuit had the American Arctic to themselves. But European exploration was about to begin again in earnest, and before long the Scandinavians were back in Greenland to stay.

*

I was sitting drinking coffee at the kitchen table on the morning after my arrival when a face appeared at the window, hands cupped around eyes. The face didn't see me at first so I waved in front of it. David Kristoffersen grinned. 'Hello Maleeky,' he shouted, then walked round to the front door and let himself in. 'Home sweet home,' David laughed, looking around the tiny room. I made more coffee and we sat down together at the table, gazing out at the ice in the bay.

David is the curator of Nanortalik's museum. A small man, smiling and fidgety, with a baseball cap permanently attached to his head, he had introduced himself to me the day before, recognising me immediately as the only tourist in town. 'Kristoffersen,' he said. 'Like the American singer.'

Although David's English is certainly better than my Danish, when we met previously I had made the mistake of explaining that I had lived in Copenhagen for six months as a student, but that I had forgotten most of what I knew of the language. It is an explanation that I have practised in Danish so many times that my ineptitude is apparently no longer convincing. Each time I used it in Greenland, English was immediately abandoned, as though false modesty alone was preventing me from communicating. And so David began to talk. Hesitantly at first – the pained, puzzled looks on my face slowing him down just now and again – but with increasing pace and enthusiasm, he spoke. Despite my minimal comprehension, I was aided by the fact that he was the most exuberant speaker I have ever met. He would stand suddenly in the middle of a sentence, as though what he was saying could not properly be expressed from a seated position. His hands held out before him, he would point at his chest and then hurl his arms outwards with his words. It was exhausting to watch, but it did help. A little.

David explained that his great-grandparents had come to Nanortalik from remote southeast Greenland to have their children christened. They knew about the religion from Moravian missionaries, and had decided that they should convert. 'That is why I am David Samuel Joseph,' he said. 'We must have Christian names, not Greenlandic names.' Many people migrated from the east coast and the Cape Farewell region to settlements around Nanortalik during the nineteenth century. Previously they had visited trading stations in the area only occasionally, but eventually they began to settle on a permanent basis. By the beginning of the twentieth century, southeast Greenland was entirely depopulated.

During a prolonged pause in the conversation, David examined the map I had spread out on the table. He seemed at first not to recognise his own town, turning the paper this way and that with a slightly uncertain look, but soon he nodded as the shapes and names began to make sense.

He pressed his forefinger to the paper and began to speak the Greenlandic place-names aloud, inviting me to repeat them. I tried my best, but he was a strict teacher and every mistake was corrected. The sounds were not easy. There is an odd, almost lisping effect in Greenlandic – a sound produced, I think, by pushing air around the sides of the tongue rather than over the top. The glottal Qs are awkward too, half-swallowed into the gullet, almost gulped down. For an English speaker these are not comfortable noises to make, but David insisted, so we continued. He tried to explain the meanings of some of the names too, pronouncing them first, then offering definitions when he was able: 'Nanor: ice bear; talik: the place where it is'. Other words were acted out. One, described partly in Greenlandic, was accompanied by a physical demonstration that suggested nothing less than a chronic bout of diarrhoea. My bewildered expression prompted him to persist with the action, becoming increasingly graphic until I could no longer imagine anything else he might be referring to. When I laughed, he laughed too, and raised his thumb to indicate that I had got it right.

Later that morning I walked back and forth through the dusty streets of the village, among houses and apartment blocks that sit up, away from the water. Most of these houses are small, with perhaps only one bedroom. They are basic, rectangular boxes, raised slightly above the ground, with steep roofs and metal chimneys. There is little to distinguish them one from the other, except for the colour of the paint and the varying states of disrepair. There are few cars in Nanortalik – there is nowhere to drive beyond the confines of the town – and people were out walking, alone or in couples. Away from the supermarkets, which stand opposite each other on the main street, the place felt quiet. No hum of industry, no traffic. Later in the day, when school was finished, children appeared, playing along the shore and among the buildings, their toys and bicycles picked up and then abandoned wherever the afternoon carried them.

Travellers often complain of the untidiness of Greenlandic towns; they are described as squalid or chaotic. But the root of this impression is not simply the human detritus, it is the non-human disorder that is found there. It is the wild land that laps up against the buildings. Bare rock is not covered here as it would be in a European town; hills and slopes are not smoothed or flattened. In between the houses is empty, uncivilised space – rocks, earth, grass, growth. There are very few gardens, and these are almost never partitioned or fenced off. People walk between the buildings, creating dusty paths with the regularity of their footsteps. Elsewhere, this between-space would always be allocated to one person or another, but in Greenland there is no private land ownership. All land belongs collectively to the state, and therefore to all people. Public space, wild space, is both out there and here, in the village. The wild is part of the community, it dwells among the houses; but the community, too, dwells within the wild. In the industrialised world we imagine a division between nature and culture, country and town, wild and domestic. We may allow a park to smudge the lines a little, or permit a river to run feral through a city, but we still see that division and that fence between. Here, the line that separates nature and culture has been erased completely. The wild roams freely in the streets.

The crucial difference between these two attitudes has nothing to do with towns and streets though, it has to do with fields and furrows. For ours is, at its root, an agricultural society, and has been for thousands of years. The Inuit, in contrast, have a hunting society. Land ownership and land division are fundamental to agriculture. Our ground is claimed, marked out and used; it is changed and dominated. We impose ourselves upon it, and we alter it to suit our will. For a hunting culture, the ownership of land simply does not make sense. Land is part of the space they inhabit, like air and water and ice; its ownership, in the private sense, is meaningless. A hunter may have rights of use in a particular area, but he no more owns the land than he owns the animals that live upon it.

The relationship is better described as one of belonging. The Greenlandic politician, Aqqaluk Lynge, has explained that 'we live there, together, therefore the land belongs to us, all of us'. But this is a reciprocal belonging: the land belongs to us, and we to it. And there, I think, is the essential disparity between the agricultural and the hunting view. The hunter sees himself as part of a natural order; he adapts to his landscape, and he accepts his place within that landscape. His aim, in Barry Lopez's words, is 'to achieve congruence with a reality that is already given'. Whereas, in our own culture, 'We hold in higher regard the land's tractability, its alterability'. The farmer, for the most part, does not adapt to his landscape, he adapts the landscape to suit his own needs. Nature is tamed, fenced off and altered. This is the attitude of the coloniser. It is the attitude with which the Norse arrived 1,000 years ago, and it is the attitude with which they died 500 years later. The Inuit have always been at home in Greenland, in a way that Europeans have never quite learned to be. They moulded their way of life around the challenges and the opportunities that the place provided. They wedded themselves to the place.

The conflict between the Inuit attitude to the land and that of Europeans is instructive, and it has significant consequences in terms of land rights, and particularly mineral rights, which Greenland currently shares with Denmark. There are a growing number of foreign companies eager to dig things out of Greenlandic ground, and the social and economic future of the country may well depend on how it chooses to deal with this situation. The trade in northern treasure, which began with the furs and narwhal tusks of the Vikings, is now more important than ever. The south still wants what the north can provide. Today, though, that treasure comes from the earth; graphite, rare metals and gold are already being mined, and there is pressure on the country to relax its ban on the extraction of uranium. The oil industry too is coming.

Many see this as an ideal solution to Greenland's economic uncertainties; it is a guaranteed income, with employment opportunities into the bargain. Others, though, are not so sure. Sheila Watt-Cloutier, a Canadian former president of the Inuit Circumpolar Conference, has called mining 'the easy way out'. She has warned that 'It could run counter to everything we are trying to recover in our culture. We need to step back and ask ourselves what kind of society we are hoping to create here. Will we lose awareness of how sacred the land is, and our connection to it? . . . Do we want to lose the wise culture we have relied on for generations?'

Land use is far from the only arena in which fundamental cultural differences have been fought out here in Greenland. As I wandered down by the harbour, old men sat outside the little shack that served as meat and fish market, smoking, laughing and talking. Some held their walking sticks in front of them, palms clasped around the handles, quietly watching the afternoon pass by. Others leaned in close towards each other, their stories told in whispers. In Qaqortoq I had seen this too, a gathering of people near the water, as if this place, where seals and fish were brought to be cut up and sold, were the social hub of the town. I imagined the men had once been hunters themselves, and now the closest they could get was to come and watch the day's catch being brought in. But the stories they were telling would connect them to those who today were wielding knives. Those stories, and the memory they contained, would connect them too to their fathers and their grandfathers, whose own knives carved into the meat, the seals, taken from the ice. These men were witnesses to a silent inheritance, a deep flash of blade and blood.

Hunting in Greenland is an issue of identity and an issue of culture. It is also an issue of very serious controversy. In particular, the killing of sea mammals – seals and whales – has for decades attracted criticism from outside. In the 1970s, following the global backlash against the killing of seal pups in Canada, Greenland's seal fur industry collapsed. The livelihood of the country's hunters was severely threatened, and so Greenland's Home Rule government stepped in to offer a solution. It nationalised the fur company, Great Greenland, and began offering a guaranteed price to hunters for every skin. It was a bold decision which, ultimately, was nothing to do with economics and everything to do with tradition. Today, while hunting is not a particularly rewarding career choice from a financial perspective, it does still remain a choice.

There is a belief among many Greenlanders that their traditional way of life – a way of life that entirely underpins their sense of identity – is under constant threat from the ignorant views of people from outside their country. A kind of moral imperialism is suspected – the imposition of alien values onto a people for whom those values do not make sense. Individuals such as Finn Lynge, a politician who in 1985 negotiated Greenland's tactical exit from the European Community, have worked hard to convince the world that the traditional Inuit culture is entirely compatible with environmental sustainability. Others have argued that the increasing European and American focus on 'animal rights', is born not from an increased empathy and understanding for the natural world but entirely the opposite. The Canadian activist Alan Herscovici has written that 'the animal-rights philosophy [is] widening rather than healing the rift between man and nature . . . [it] may be more of a symptom of our disease than a cure.'

Lynge would agree. For him, the focus on individual animals' rights demonstrates a failure to understand nature, or to recognise our own place within it. What the Inuit see in the European and American attitudes to Arctic hunting is the gaping distance between our people and our environment. They see a hypocritical culture that frets and recoils over the deaths of individual animals elsewhere in the world, yet which engages in industrial farming, 'pest-control' on an immense scale, widespread polluting and the devastating destruction of natural habitats. As individuals, we consciously distance ourselves from killing, we close our eyes to it, yet our culture is, in general, 'characterized by its propensity for cruelty and death', as Lynge has it. And our distaste for hunting is a very recent development.

As a teenager I knew men who had been whalers. Shetland has always had a strong connection with that industry. As Herman Melville noted in *Moby Dick*, 'the Greenland whalers sailing out of Hull or London, put in at the Shetland Islands, to receive the full complement of their crew. Upon the passage homewards, they drop them there again. How it is, there is no telling, but Islanders seem to make the best whalemen.'

From the seventeenth to the nineteenth century, thousands of Shetland men sailed west to Greenland, leaving wives and mothers to look after the crofts in the islands. They would return months later with more money than could ever be earned at home. By the twentieth century, though, the industry had moved to the south Atlantic, based around the island of South Georgia. Again, many Shetlanders travelled the length of the ocean to work, to kill whales. I would listen to the stories these men told – men not much older than my father – and I could barely believe that they could have lived such a life, that these things could have taken place so recently. It seemed incredible, like another world, so quickly have we distanced ourselves from whale hunting.

It is easy to understand why the Inuit see hypocrisy in the European attitude to whaling. Britain and others led an intense industrial assault on the whale for centuries, an assault that ended only in the 1960s, when that industry ceased to be profitable. And today, the pollutants we pump into the air and sea are far more of a threat to Arctic wildlife than the hunters who live there. So the moral high-ground, from which we lecture on the evils of killing sea mammals, seems at least a little shaky. For if these animals are now endangered – and some species certainly are – the blame lies not with the Inuit but at our own door.

It would be a mistake, though, to dismiss concerns about hunting entirely. Wildlife in the Arctic is vulnerable, and the needless killing of animals and birds in Greenland has been well documented, both historically and in the present day. Today, some claim, hunting regulations are routinely flouted and rarely enforced, and populations of some bird species, such as Brünnich's guillemots and eider ducks, are well below sustainable levels. Lynge and others have been accused of misrepresenting the truth, and of propagating 'the myth of the sustainable Inuit'.

It is commonly agreed, however, even among groups such as Greenpeace, who led the anti-sealing campaigns of the 1970s, that Greenland's seal hunt is not damaging the animals' population. Numbers of the four main species – ringed, bearded, harp and hooded seals – are stable or rising, and there is little prospect of increased demand for fur threatening this balance. Watching the hunters arrive at the market each afternoon, seeing them carefully slice and distribute the meat, I was glad that this was so, glad it could continue.

One evening over dinner, a young Greenlandic couple who had invited me to their home, asked whether we had seals in Shetland. When I replied that we had many but that islanders had never really eaten them, they seemed confused.

'Why wouldn't you eat them?' the woman enquired.

I did not have a good answer. I thought, perhaps, that an abundance of fish might have made seal meat superfluous in the past, but that didn't seem very plausible. I wondered also whether superstition might have played a part. Stories of selkie folk – seal people – were widespread in Shetland as they were elsewhere in northern Scotland, and perhaps this notion that seals were somehow too human to be eaten, that they might have souls, was the real problem. I wasn't sure, and I am still not sure. The young woman seemed dissatisfied with my answer, and I was not surprised. The idea that a seal might have a soul did not seem, to her, a good reason for it not to be eaten.

A shaman once explained to the explorer and anthropologist Knud Rasmussen that 'the greatest peril lies in the fact that to kill and eat, all that we strike down and destroy . . . have souls as we have, souls that do not perish with the body, and therefore must be propitiated lest they revenge themselves.' For the traditional Inuit, souls are not the exclusive property of human beings, they are widespread and take many forms. Propitiation is achieved by following certain cultural traditions and, at all times, by showing respect towards the animal that is killed. It is both atonement and thanksgiving. In our own culture, meat has been increasingly divorced, for most of its consumers, from the death that makes it possible and the life that it once held. Because of this, there is a kind of thankfulness and humility that we no longer know how to feel, and a grace we have forgotten how to say.

*

Fat grey clouds tumbled heavily around the mountains, punctured and crushed between the peaks, rolling, blowing and inflating, from slate to black, turning over in the wind. There was rain there, on the slopes. It had not reached the town yet, but it was coming. I was stranded inside the cabin. Flu had struck me on my second day in Nanortalik, and had worsened until I felt unable to leave the warmth of the building. I was hot and shivering, my nose was blocked and sinuses throbbing; my throat was raw and my muscles ached. I felt dreadful, and sat on the sofa next to the fire looking out of the window. Hours passed slowly. I read, but found it difficult to concentrate for long. I turned on the television, but switched it off again when I saw what was there.

Outside, the ice shifted, clearing then clotting the dark water again, as the wind dragged from east to south to southwesterly. I watched its steady migration back and forth across the bay, and something inside me moved as it moved. My thoughts drifted from the island where I sat, to my own island 1,500 miles east along the parallel. I thought about the people in this town, and I thought about the great space that lay between their lives and my own. I thought, too, about my father, who seemed as close to me then as the ice outside, or the warmth within the room, but as distant and unreachable as the ravens across the bay, their black lives pinpricked against the sky.

Above the water, glaucous and Iceland gulls bustled their way between the bergs, camouflaged on the ice. As they lifted up to shift to another place now and then, they shone bright white in the grey air. Rain wrapped itself around the town then, and I opened the window a little to listen to it falling. Inland, a thick fog was slumped around the mountains, but out to sea, from where the breeze was blowing, the sky was bright. It was an illusion – the reflection of the sea ice on the clouds above – but it was welcome nonetheless, and added to the ever-present promise of change. Gretel Ehrlich has written that 'Arctic beauty resides in its gestures of transience. Up here, planes of light and darkness are swords that cut away illusions of permanence'. In Greenland, that transience is impossible to ignore; it permeates each moment of each day. It is there in the melting icebergs on the shore, and in the meat on the market counters; it is there in the rushing clouds and the changing climate. It is there in the air itself. There is the sense here that, at any moment, all certainty could be undermined – that the land could reach out in an instant and wipe people away, as the Norse were once wiped from this country. There is terror in that thought, but there is comfort, too.

When my father died I learned that loss is with us always. It is not a punctuating mark in our lives, it is not a momentary pause or ending. Loss is a constant force, a spirit that moves both within and without us. It is an unceasing process that we may choose, if we wish, to bear witness to. And if we do make that choice, then we are not committing ourselves to a lifetime of grief and melancholy. Instead, we offer ourselves the opportunity of a firmer sense of joy and of beauty. It is no surprise and certainly no coincidence that we experience our greatest appreciation of life in those things that are fragile and fleeting. We find it in the song of a bird, in the touch of a lover, or in the memory of a moment long passed. So it should be no surprise that by attuning ourselves better to the process of loss and transience, we may in turn be brought nearer to beauty and to joy. It is in loss – in the anticipation of loss – that we find our most profound pleasures, and it is there also that we may find a sense of true permanence.

In traditional Inuit society, permanence was to be found in the concept of *sila*, a kind of life force or spirit, which is sometimes translated as air, wind or weather, or, more widely still, as 'everything that is outside'. *Sila* was the essential ingredient of life – it was breath itself – and it held the inner and outer worlds together. When a person died, their life, their breath, returned to the world and became one with it again, or it found form in another person's body. But *sila* was not a predictable permanence; it was not certainty. *Sila* encompassed both weather and climate. It was changeable, surprising, and sometimes malign. Death was part of its process and part of its force, and the Inuit understanding of the world was shaped by this belief. Or perhaps it would be more true to say that the world in which the Inuit lived shaped this understanding. For natural philosophies do not spring from empty space, they are born from the land. And this seems to me a particularly northern view of life and death. Here, where the seasons turn heavily, emphatically, and where impermanence cannot be disguised, *sila*, somehow, makes sense.

Death is at once an ending and a continuation. A breath is given back to the wind, just as ice returns to the sea. It finds new shape. But a life, too, lives on through stories and through memories, joyful in their retelling and their fleeting recollection. Loss shapes us like a sculptor, carving out our form, and we feel each nick of its blade. But without it we cannot be. Of the many absences that I carry with me – for we all, I think, are filled with holes – the absence of my father is the one that has taught me most. It is the space through which I have come to see myself most clearly. I thought of him then, as an ice-laden wind pawed at the cabin window, and I thought of myself in those first few months without him. His was the loss that had led me to this place.

*

It was another two days before I felt well enough to venture out beyond the shelter of the hostel again. My strength had drained in the stifling heat inside, and I needed to walk. The morning was dry and calm, and so I aimed for Quaqssuk – Ravens' Mountain – which rose just beyond the north end of the village. Nanortalik's main street was filled with teenagers that morning, just finished their final term at junior high school. They were dressed in white T-shirts, all painted with slogans and pictures, or printed with photographs of their friends and classmates. Spray cream was everywhere, and treacle too, on their hands and faces. They were chanting a song like a football anthem, and smiling as they went. Cars beeped and people cheered in congratulation.

Much earlier in the day, at five or six a.m., the rabble would have been prowling the streets, dragging tin cans on strings behind them, banging metal trays and yelling loudly outside the homes of their teachers. In Narsaq, further up the coast, I had seen (or at least heard) the same ritual, and wondered at first if some kind of early morning riot was unfolding. But this was an annual event, I was told. It was a ceremony, marking the end of one part of the children's lives and their imminent entry into another. Most of them now would have to leave home, to complete high school in another town.

As I walked out on the dirt track towards Quassik, the sounds of the street faded and the sounds of the mountain grew. Lapland buntings flung themselves into the air around me, then glided back to earth again, wings outstretched, singing as they fell. Among the low bushes, redpolls danced and darted, some stopping close by to watch me pass. The air shimmered with song. Beneath my feet, the lower slopes were thick with life: crowberry, dwarf willows, tiny white flowers among the rocks, plump beds of mosses and lichens. There was, everywhere, an anticipation of summer.

It was warm as I began to climb the trail, and I soon took off my jacket, then my jumper. The walking wasn't difficult, but after three days lying down I wasn't feeling fit. It took an hour to gain the steep 300 metres to the top of the hill, and just a few more minutes from the first cairned summit to the highest point, topped by a pyramid of stones. The view was astonishing. To the north and east, snow-studded mountains rose abruptly from the fjords, all cluttered with ice. Peak after ragged peak stood whisped in haze and shadows. Behind me was the town, looking tiny and worn out, its colour drained by distance. Beyond it, to the south and west, was the straight line where the sea ice began, a carpet of white and blue and light, with only a few huge bergs protruding above the flat surface.

I sat down on a rock just north of the peak and ate my lunch. There was only a hint of a breeze, and everything was close to silence. The far-off hum of a helicopter; the drone of a bluebottle nearby; an outboard motor, somewhere among the fjords. Besides these, the only sound was the whispering of air among the mountains, a kind of live white noise.

I lay back with my head on the lichen crust of the rocks. The sun was only just breaking through now as the cloud slowly thickened, but it was still warm on my skin. I listened to the quiet and closed my eyes. There is great pleasure to be had in lying down outside. On a sun-drenched beach or a cold Shetland hillside, wrapped up warm or in shorts and a T-shirt, a doze in the open air is rarely a bad idea. Wild sleeping is as rejuvenating an activity as wild swimming, and it has the major benefit of being a lot less wet. I think my fondness for the activity – if you can call it an activity – in part explains why I am such a poor mountaineer. The lure of the summit is rarely strong enough to lead me further than a good view and a comfortable napping spot, and unless I can combine the two goals, such as here on Quassik, recumbency usually wins out. On this occasion, though, I didn't sleep long. Almost as soon as I had closed my eyes, something changed. I felt a breeze on my face – a sudden gust from the north that failed to fall away – and the temperature dropped. Even with my eyes shut I could sense a darkening of the sky. So I decided to move.

The walk back down the slope was easy and enjoyable, and the threatened downpour failed to materialise. I made my way into the village again, through the ramshackle streets of its eastern edge, but I was stopped by a loud voice calling. A man was beckoning me from his open window,

Danish rock music pouring out from behind him. I couldn't understand what the man was shouting, nor could I see the expression on his face, friendly or angry. But he stretched his arm in my direction and called me over, so I moved, somewhat reluctantly, towards him.

'Dansk?' he asked, when I was close enough to comprehend.

'Nej, Engelsk,' I responded, for simplicity's sake.

'Where are you from?' he said slowly, in English.

'From Scotland,' I answered, a little more accurately this time.

'Scotland, yes,' he smiled. This was clearly a welcome answer, for the man immediately invited me in to his house, and sat me down opposite him by the window. An open can of beer stood between us on the table. 'I am Thomas,' he said, then elaborated. 'Thomas Jefferson – you know? – the United States' president. That was not me!'

He laughed, then lapsed back into Danish, where he remained for the rest of the conversation. I tried my best to follow.

He told me he was a pensioner, though he was only 57 years old. He used to be a sailor, working on the ferry between Esbjerg in Denmark and Harwich in England, but now he was retired. This was his house, he said, but he didn't really live here; he lived with his mother. There was a photo of her on the wall, which he pointed out to me with pride. He lived with his mother, but he came to this house during the day to listen to music and to get drunk. In the summertime he went hunting and fishing in his boat, and sometimes he took tourists up the fjord. But for now, it seemed, the next can was as far as he was going.

A big man, with a slight limp, and a face that smiled even when his mouth did not, Thomas was, I thought, somewhat shy, though alcohol had brought him confidence. His exuberance was not really talkativeness either, just enthusiasm for sharing a moment; and like many of the Greenlanders I met, his conversation was punctuated by long, silent gazes out of the window.

Thomas was not the only person in town who spent his days with a beer in front of him. I was visited at the cabin on more than one occasion by men some considerable distance from sobriety. They were always polite and quiet, but still I was disconcerted by these uninvited guests. Alcoholism in Greenland, as in many Arctic communities, is a major problem among the native population. More recently, drug and solvent abuse have also become serious issues, along with a rise in teenage pregnancy and in health problems such as obesity. The reason, in part, is poverty, and a lack of education. But it goes deeper than that.

In Narsaq, two weeks earlier, I had spoken to Bolethe Stenskov, a social worker and counsellor, who told me that the country was suffering from the problems of rapid social change. 'We have moved from being hunters to modern life very quickly,' she said. In just a few decades a massive cultural transition has been made, and it has not been an easy one. Low self-esteem is a particularly significant problem, she explained, especially among men, who find themselves without their traditional community status. Once they were hunters, providing for their family. Now it is much harder for them to find a role. Capitalism has introduced a new set of values to Inuit culture – a framework of indulgence – and while Western materialism has yet to be fully embraced, our compulsive consumption has been adopted in an altogether damaging way. Alcohol, drugs, tobacco, junk food: this is non-accumulative consumption. It is our own excess, translated into Greenlandic.

Bolethe offers support, advice and information to those who need it, and despite her familiarity with the problems, she maintains a remarkably positive outlook. She sees her job as, unfortunately, a necessary one within this society.

The damaging cycles of addiction, of abuse and ill-health, passed down between generations, cannot be broken without intervention. And key to that intervention, Bolethe believes, must be education, for both children and adults. Currently, many youngsters struggle in school. They struggle because their parents may be unable to help them, or unwilling to encourage them. They may have a Danish teacher, but may not have the necessary skills in that language to carry them along. There is, too, a shortage of positive role models among the adult population. These factors can easily lead to a lack of interest in education, and a failure to connect with the learning process. But if they are to find a meaningful place for themselves within society, as it exists today, they must make that connection.

There is a paradox here, though, as there is in many traditional societies. For Greenlandic culture is deeply woven together with the idea of place, and the community is central within people's lives. Yet with each step in the education process, and with each successful progression, children are likely to find themselves drawn further and further away from their place and their community. At fifteen, they must leave home to complete high school elsewhere. Then, if they wish to go further, to college or university, they must go to Nuuk or to Copenhagen. These students must travel far from home, and that distance will not just be geographical. Almost as soon as they enter the education system, children are already leaving behind the traditional knowledge of their grandparents, and the higher they climb the greater that distance will become. Education promises choice and opportunities, but in return it asks for aspirations and ambition. These aspirations are rarely compatible with a small Greenlandic community; they are rarely compatible with a life that maintains a real connection to culture and tradition. There is much to be lost here – much that has already been lost elsewhere – and while education represents an opportunity, it also potentially poses a threat.

When I put this to Bolethe, though, she disagreed. There is no contradiction, she told me. 'We need to improve education and quality of life, but also retain our culture as hunting people.' So how is that possible, I asked. How do you retain a culture that is, at its heart, at odds with the education system and with the economic system that education underpins? Bolethe smiled and looked out of the window. She lifted her hand and gestured out towards the harbour, the ice and the mountains across the fjord. The answer was simple, she said. 'We have the nature; we have the landscape and the sea. There is our culture. It is with us.'

I looked out and tried to muster the same confidence. I tried to persuade myself that Bolethe was correct. Here in Greenland, as elsewhere on the parallel, the landscape and climate continue to bring the same challenges they always have. The place continues to make demands upon the people. And while individuals might struggle to reshape themselves as society changed, perhaps the culture would still yield to those demands. I hoped it was so. I hoped that she was right.

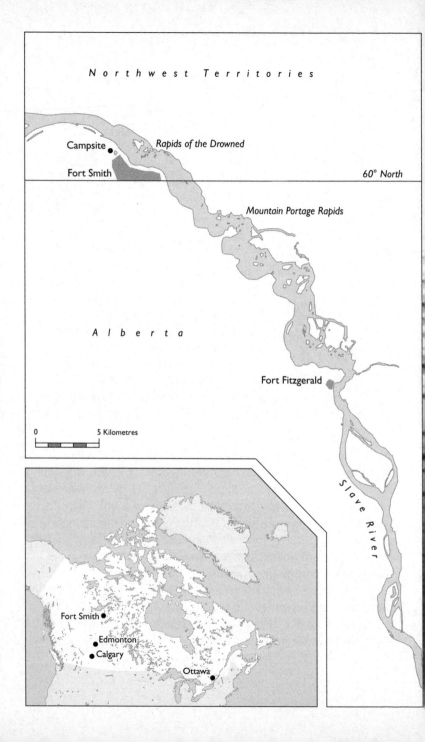

CANADA
beside the rapids

No other nation has worked as hard to understand, define and come to terms with the north as Canada. And no other nation, surely, has such an inconsistent relationship with that place, which it both contains and embodies. Canada is a northern country and sees itself as such, particularly in relation to the United States. Around forty percent of its landmass lies north of sixty degrees – a vast area, comparable in size to the entire European Union. And yet the country's centre of balance is firmly in the south. The population – around 33 million in total – is concentrated along the southern border, and the most northerly city of more than half a million people is Edmonton, just above fifty-three degrees, the same latitude as Dublin. Only about 100,000 Canadians actually live above the sixtieth parallel – considerably fewer, in fact, than Americans.

For most in Canada, then, the north remains alien, a neighbour but a stranger. Many dream of it, but few ever wake up there. It is a place read about in books, seen in films and on television, but rarely visited. Viewed from afar, the region is tangled in contradictions. North means danger and adventure, but it also means refuge. It offers possibility and fear, beauty and horror. It is almost empty of people and yet overflowing with their imaginings.

But for those who do wish to know the north, and to see it for themselves, the first difficulty is getting there, for the north is nearly always beyond the horizon. I arrived in the country in Calgary, Alberta, and my destination was the town of Fort Smith, just inside the Northwest Territories. It was a twenty-four hour coach ride away.

A cluster of tall buildings raised like an exclamation in the flat prairie, Calgary was bathed in summer heat that afternoon. As always, my fear of flying had left me unable to sleep while in the air, and the time change had made things worse. By eight p.m., when the Greyhound bus pulled out of the depot into the clean sunlight of the streets, it had been a very long time since I had last been asleep. We drove north from the city and into the broad plains beyond. In the west, clouds were piled like rubble above the Rocky Mountains, haze-drawn on the horizon. The bus was filled with chatter, but outside the soft light of the evening lay like a blanket of quiet upon the fields.

Our first stop was Red Deer, shortly before ten p.m., just as the sun was setting. My head was cluttered with half-formed, exhausted thoughts, but I held myself awake, staring dazedly through the window. As we continued towards Edmonton an hour passed, but the memory of the sun lingered. Colours washed out, leaving behind a muted light; and as the sky softened to golden grey in the northwest, farmhouses dissolved into silhouettes – fat, black stains on the disappearing land.

At Edmonton we changed buses. It was midnight, but the depot was still full of people. Many of the passengers had brought pillows and blankets with them, and as we drove on into the darkness, voices settled into silence. I bundled up my jacket, then wedged it between the seatback and the window. Closing my eyes, I tried to sleep.

By the time we reached the town of Slave Lake at three a.m., a smear of white was in the northeast sky. Soon after, darkness began to lift again. Trees emerged from the night, close against the road, blocking the view beyond. An hour or so later the prairie returned, with fields stretched out in every direction. The farms were tidy – all straight lines and well-kept gardens, quaint wooden houses and giant grain silos. Even the old cars had been abandoned in neat rows, lined up, perhaps, in the order in which they stopped working. A few white-tailed deer grazed here and there, and once the driver blew his horn at a pair that strayed into the road. The deer were forced into a quick decision, the right decision.

The journey north – in history, in literature, in the imagination – is a journey away from the centres of civilisation and culture, towards the unknown and the other. Margaret Atwood has written that, 'Turning to . . . face the north, we enter our own unconscious. Always, in retrospect, the journey north has the quality of a dream'. Looking out through the tinted windows of the coach, my own journey felt dreamlike. But it was not my own dream. Rather, it was as though someone else's unconscious were being projected against the glass. The honeyed light of the early morning, the procession of fields, farms, trees and towns, all seemed remote and unreal somehow. I felt disorientated and disconnected from the place outside. I observed but couldn't engage. I let the morning wash over me, hour after hour.

In 1964, the pianist Glenn Gould travelled on the Muskeg Express, a thousand-mile train journey lasting a day and two nights, from Winnipeg to Churchill, on the shores of Hudson Bay. It was his first northern journey, and on his return Gould made a radio programme about the trip. *The Idea of North* is not a documentary in any conventional sense; it is a collage of voices. Using interviews with a civil servant, a geographer, a nurse and a sociologist, all with experience of northern Canada, as well as a narrator of sorts called Wally Maclean, Gould created, to use his word, a 'contrapuntal' picture of the north. Like a choir of competing melodies, these voices rise, tumble and are lost. Ideas emerge then vanish again, as though glimpsed from a moving train. Sometimes they come through clearly, with only the gentle clunk and clatter of the tracks in the background; other times the sounds overlap, with voices jostling for the listener's attention. Towards the programme's end the last movement of Sibelius's Fifth Symphony begins, and soon it rears up above Maclean's closing monologue, threatening to overwhelm his words, until at last there is only silence.

Going north to me means going home, and every journey I take in this direction brings with it the feeling of return. Once that feeling was an unwelcome one, reminding me always of the times I made it when I didn't wish to do so. But that has changed. It was two years after I was brought back to Shetland, aged sixteen and fatherless, that I found another way out, and another way forward. In that time, I suppose, I'd come to understand that, wherever I went from then on, Shetland would be the place to which I returned. I no longer had close family or friends elsewhere; I no longer had much to connect me with anywhere except the islands. My centre of gravity had shifted north, and though I didn't yet feel its pull, I knew that change had taken place.

It was without a great deal of enthusiasm that I decided, eventually, to go to university. Others were going, and it made sense for me to go too. It was a logical escape route. But a handful of mediocre exam results from my last year at school were not enough to get me anywhere, and so I enrolled in night-classes and took more exams. Further mediocre results followed. In the end I managed to persuade one university to take me, based on the quantity rather than the quality of my grades, I suppose. And it was my good fortune that they did, because I enjoyed almost every moment of those four years, from arrival until graduation, and I thrived there in a way that I'd failed to do at school. It was during those years in Scotland that I began to look north when I thought of home, and even to feel relief at holiday times as the train took me back up the country, towards the ferry, and a night on the North Sea.

*

It was a little after six a.m. when we descended into the Peace Valley. No one had spoken for three hours, though a few, like me, had sat awake throughout the night. In Peace River, dazed and dazzled, we had a break. Given ninety minutes in which to fill our stomachs and stretch our legs, I took a short walk through the centre of town, then went for coffee and breakfast in Rusty's Diner. It was just me and the waitress. A pile of steaming pancakes arrived, doused with maple syrup, and I ate them greedily, enjoying every mouthful. I felt almost refreshed.

When the time came to continue, only seven of us got back on the bus. It was raining heavily then, and we trundled into a changing landscape. Though we were still among the prairies, the agriculture was less intensive, the farms smaller, the roads less straight. Land space was shared about evenly between fields of cattle or fodder, and light, mostly deciduous woodland. In places, cows grazed among the trees.

In this country there are a multitude of lines and frontiers behind which lies the north. These frontiers have cultural and political, as well as geographical, significance, and much effort has been expended locating them. On a map it's possible to draw a series of boundaries and borders between north and south, or between 'near' and 'far north'. There is the tree line, above which the boreal forest gives way to tundra; the southern limit of permafrost; the Arctic Circle; the sixtieth parallel. Other measurements are also made. Temperature, precipitation, accessibility, population density: all are calculated, and a level of 'nordicity' can be assigned, according to a scale developed in the 1970s by the geographer Louis-Edmond Hamelin.

For scientists, politicians and civil servants, such measurements are useful. They allow direct, accurate comparisons of environmental and social situations across the country.

But there is a problem. Nordicity is a southern concept – an attempt to contain what cannot truly be held – and the criteria by which it is assessed are not really measurements of northernness (other than latitude, of course); they are measurements of cold, isolation, inaccessibility and foreignness. In other words, they are calculations of how places correspond to a preconceived notion of what the north ought to be, epitomised by that most foreign of all earthly places, the North Pole. So Hamelin could write of 'a 25% denordification across the North [over the past century]', as though by changing, by developing, by warming, the north can actually become less like itself.

The view from inside, though, is different. The north is all that it contains. It is a place capable of change and diversity, a place immeasurable. It holds the preconceived, yes, but also the unimagined and the unimaginable. Above all else, for those who live there, the north is home. It is neither remote nor isolated nor far away; it is the centre of the world. For me, the very arbitrariness of the sixtieth parallel, its total lack of what Hamelin called 'natural relevance', is its great advantage, making it an ideal place along which to explore the north. For the parallel is not a line by which to measure anything quantitatively, nor is it a clear border between one place and another. Instead, the parallel is entirely undefining. It allows for a plurality of norths to exist.

By mid-morning there were only trees – birch, spruce, trembling aspen, tamarack, balsam poplar – and a narrow space on either side of the road. Here and there a stretch of swampy ground emerged from the forest, or a lake, often with a beaver's lodge or two tucked up against the bank. The rain had stopped and the sky cleared by then, and the day was swollen with sunshine. I watched the trees, half-hypnotised, and thought about what lay beyond this parting of the forest. Out there, away from the road's slender imposition, lay the whole country, and more. This immense

Canada

boreal forest, of taiga and muskeg, stretches across northern Canada and Alaska, then on through Siberia, the Urals and into Scandinavia, tying the top of the planet together. It is easy to imagine stepping out among the trees here and walking within their shadow, until you emerge somewhere else entirely, some other part of the north. Except of course that you wouldn't. More likely, the person who stepped into the forest, unless they truly knew this place, would become disorientated immediately, then they would be lost, and sooner or later they would die. Nature here is a contradictory presence. It is abundant and overflowing with life, and yet threatening and hostile to our intrusions. The forest is the road's antithesis. We no longer know how to live with it, and so we pass quickly through, on our way to another clearing.

The highway carried few vehicles. Every ten minutes or so a pickup went by, or sometimes a truck, and once a yellow school bus appeared like a daydream, then was gone. The hours passed, and morning became afternoon. We stopped for lunch at High Level, with its ugly strip of motels, bars and fast food restaurants, then the insect-choked gas station at Indian Cabins. At half past two we crossed the sixtieth parallel and the border into the Northwest Territories. Only three of us remained. For mile after mile nothing changed, the view appeared identical. We turned a corner and we might as well not have moved. It was as though there were nowhere else left but the forest.

The Greyhound reached Hay River, the end of its line, at four p.m. The tiny, dusty depot seemed intensely hot, and a shock after the air-conditioned coach. When the time came for the minibus to depart fifteen minutes later, I was the only passenger taking the 170-mile trip southeast to Fort Smith. (In the north, distances between towns are often so great that it makes more sense to measure them in hours than in miles. This would be a three-hour journey, with no stops between here and there.) My driver, Andrew, insisted that I come and sit up in the front with him so that he could 'give me the tour'. As we set off, Andrew explained that he was partially deaf, so I would have to speak clearly and face in his direction. This partial deafness also required him to talk just a little too insistently throughout, as though he suspected I might be doubting every word he said.

We began the drive with the kind of tales I had been hoping not to hear. For my entertainment, Andrew recounted in detail the stories of two fatal bear attacks in the region. The first of these was a driver who had crashed his vehicle on this very road, then attracted the bear's attention by lying at the roadside bleeding. He was found too late, halfway through being consumed. The second attack involved a couple from Hay River who were camping beside Great Slave Lake. Needless to say, they never came home. It seemed there were a lot of bears around here. In fact, the last time Andrew made this trip he'd seen six of them between the two towns. I tried to look impressed, or at least unafraid, but it was hard. I was thinking about the little tent in my bag, in which I'd intended to sleep.

'I'm a bit nervous about bears, actually,' I admitted. Andrew turned to me, unsure whether I was joking or not. 'Oh, you don't need to be nervous,' he said, when he saw that I was serious. 'You'll be fine.' While this reassurance was not entirely adequate, I was relieved to learn that the animals in this area were black rather than brown bears. Smaller, less aggressive, more easily deterred, they were a safer kind of bear all round. And though they did kill people once in a while, it was rather more unusual an occurrence than Andrew's stories might have led me to believe. As he said, I would probably be fine.

When Andrew pressed his foot to the brake, he was mid-sentence and mid-sandwich. 'Buffalo,' he spat, pointing up ahead. The animals were impossible to miss. A group of six, some standing, some rolling in the dust at the roadside, the creatures were enormous, and unconcerned as we slowed almost to a stop just a few metres away. They were strange beasts – their back-ends like cattle, but their front halves and heads like something else entirely: broad, dark, woolly, bearded and horned, they looked like relics of another age. The adults stood well over six feet tall at their humped shoulders, with the large males weighing in at up to a ton. The youngsters were lighter in colour, and not dissimilar to the calves of domestic cattle. These wood buffalo are the largest land mammals in North America, one of two sub-species of the American bison that once roamed the Great Plains in their tens of millions, and which were slaughtered almost to extinction.

For most of this journey from Hay River to Fort Smith we were driving through Wood Buffalo National Park, a UNESCO World Heritage Site and, at 17,300 square miles, the second largest protected area in the world, after North-east Greenland. The park was established in 1922 to help protect one of the last existing herds of free-roaming wood bison, and today there are around 5,000 of them in the area. Like many large animals, the bison appeared weighed down by their own bulk, and seemed to live at a slower pace than other creatures. They lumbered unhurriedly across and alongside the road, apparently oblivious to the vehicle in their midst. Flies clouded around their backs and heads in thick, sickening swarms, but even their short tails swished and swatted the insects at half speed. Over the next hour we saw another thirty or forty bison, some in groups, others alone, and each time they were somehow unbelievable. And then there was something different.

A black mark beside the road, a hundred yards ahead. A boulder-sized shape that came to life as we approached. A shape that lifted its head, unfurled itself, and became a bear. This time it was me who alerted Andrew. The bear stood and watched the vehicle as we slowed down. It was not a large animal – perhaps only a year or two old – but it seemed confident, and held still for a long time, not moving until we'd drawn up almost alongside it. The eyes peered at us, perhaps assessing the threat, and we stared back, safe within our box of glass and metal. But at the precise moment we came to a stop, the bear turned, moving without much haste back into the forest. We drove on in silence.

Andrew dropped me at the campsite just outside Fort Smith. There was no one else around. I wandered among the lanky jack pines looking for a flat, sheltered spot on which to put up my tent, then struggled, in bursts of rage and frustration, to put the pieces together and press the pegs into the ground. A difficult job was made harder by mosquitoes and exhaustion, and I scratched at my face and neck, half-hallucinating in the warm, evening air. I was weak and dizzy, and my eyes hurt when I tried to concentrate. It had been almost forty-eight hours since I last slept. Fatigue flooded over me as I crawled inside the tent and lay down with my head upon my jacket. A slight nausea rose too, as though to engulf my whole body, then it slipped away like a sigh and was gone. I felt entirely alone, then, yet too tired to be lonely. I felt exhilarated, briefly, to be there in the forest. And then I was asleep.

*

Moving through this country has always been difficult. Dense forest, boggy ground, extreme temperatures and hostile insect life: the early European travellers found their way slowed by innumerable dangers. The most convenient means of travel, historically, has been to step off the land altogether and to get on the water, and lakes and rivers have long been the highways of the north, reliable for paddling in summer and for sledging and walking in winter. In 1789, the Scottish-born explorer Alexander Mackenzie was searching for a northern route to the Pacific Ocean, but found something else instead. Making his way from Lake Athabasca, in what is now northern Alberta and Saskatchewan, north along the Slave River to the Great Slave Lake, then onwards along a second, much longer river to the Arctic Ocean, he opened up what was to become one of the great Canadian trading routes. That second river, which he named 'Disappointment' upon reaching its end, is now called the Mackenzie, and is the longest river lying entirely within Canada.

That route to the Arctic was to become immensely important over the next two centuries, providing a reliable means of reaching northern communities for the missionaries and traders who travelled the region. The great advantage of this particular route was its simplicity. Over the entire 1,500 miles between Lake Athabasca and the Arctic, there was only one major obstacle to transport. Halfway along the Slave River, just as it crosses the sixtieth parallel, four huge sets of rapids churn the water into a riotous wash of foaming white and brown. High waves, deep holes and hidden rocks combine to make much of this seventeen-mile stretch entirely impassable by boat.

Today, sections of these rapids provide some of the most challenging and exciting water in the world for kayakers and canoeists, but in the past travellers had to do their best to avoid the danger. That meant getting out of the river. Since before the first Europeans ever reached this place, a series of portage routes existed, and these were gradually developed as people made the journey more regularly. By the early nineteenth century, larger vessels had come into use, and they too had to be hauled out, requiring incredible effort. This was particularly true at Mountain Rapids, where the portage involved a precipitous climb of 75 feet, then an equally steep descent back to the river. A winch system made it possible, but certainly not easy. The travellers, however, had no choice; the river was simply too treacherous to follow. And for any voyager who might have been tempted to risk the water, there was a constant reminder of the potential dangers. For below the first three sets of rapids – today known as Cassette, Pelican and Mountain – lies the last, called then, as now, the Rapids of the Drowned. The name, coined after an accident in 1786 in which five men lost their lives, served as both a memorial and as a warning to others.

During the late nineteenth century, the Hudson's Bay Company established two small settlements on the west bank of the river, one at either end of the portage system. At Cassette Rapids was Smith's Landing (now called Fort Fitzgerald), and on a high bluff overlooking the Rapids of the Drowned was Fort Smith. When the shorter portages were eventually succeeded in the 1880s by a single, seventeen-mile trail, and steamboats began to operate on either side of the rapids, a new simplified era of transportation began. The country opened up, and changed forever. The north became accessible to anyone who wished to go there, and Fort Smith, in effect, was its gateway. The town grew rapidly. Freight companies appeared and prospered; labouring work and other employment was in plentiful supply. By 1921, it had become the administrative centre for the entire Northwest Territories.

*

It was a short walk along the highway from my campsite to the town. The air was hot and humming with insects, and I clung close to the shadows at the forest's edge, keeping out of the sun. A single vehicle passed as I walked – an old grey pickup heading west towards the airport. Other than that, the road was empty.

The first houses were large and set some way back from the road, behind wire or wooden fences. The street was wide and edged with dust and gravel, with deep ditches on either side, and a yellow-stained pavement. Some of the gardens looked unkempt, but not uncared-for, and the air smelt of pine, flowers and early summer soil. From behind one house, two small dogs came bounding, yapping fiercely as I passed, but neither would venture further than the open gate.

I had no map, and no idea where I was going. I had no plans, other than the one my stomach had made for breakfast. I followed McDougal Street, vaguely expecting a town centre to emerge, which it vaguely did: a crossroads – McDougal and Breynat Street – with Wally's drugstore on one corner, Saint Joseph Cathedral on another, and a few wooden benches on which to sit and watch the traffic. Crowded close around this junction were a library, two supermarkets, the fire station, town hall, hotel and red-brick post office, and a shop selling flowers, chocolates and coffee. Trees were lined up neatly on the lawn outside the cathedral, and extravagant hanging baskets dangled like cherries from the street lamps. On impulse I turned right onto Portage Avenue, then stopped at Kelly's gas station for something to eat and drink. I sat down in the sun with my juice and sandwich, and was joined by a gang of hungry wasps.

Virtually all of this town is squeezed into a slim stretch of land between the river and Highway 5. 'Smith', as it's referred to by residents, is home to around two and a half thousand people, but feels larger because of its isolation. It has the amenities of a much bigger place. There is a college here, a primary and a secondary school, a leisure centre and a golf club, a local paper, a few places to eat, a few bars, some churches and a museum, though very few tourists this early in the summer. The town also has a beguiling openness. People smiled and said hello to me as they passed. If I saw them a second time I was offered another smile and a nod of recognition.

The air was heavy and humid as I wandered about the streets, and a hint of thunder trembled through a black cloud in the west. A few spots of rain fell, but the pavements dried as soon as each drop touched the ground. Early in the afternoon I picked up a map from the National Park office and continued to walk, circling the town centre and exploring its edges. At some time in the mid-twentieth century, in a moment of cack-handed inspiration, many of Fort Smith's streets had been given names that not only strained towards geographical and cultural 'appropriateness' but were also, quite inexplicably, alliterative. Prior to that almost all roads had been anonymous, and in the minds of many residents most remain so. But now, officially at least, at one end of McDougal Street are Woodbison Avenue, Wilderness Road, Whipoorwill Crescent and Weasel Street, while at the other are Park Drive, Paddle Street, Portage Avenue and Pickerel, Poppy, Pine and Polar Crescents. Some of the names are sickeningly twee, such as Teepee Trail, while others are reminiscent of another place entirely – Primrose Lane could have wound its way through a tale by Beatrix Potter, but here it is a rough gravel road leading out into the forest, where a carved monument hides amid the trees to Edward Martin, 'the best woodcutter of the north'.

I returned in the late afternoon to the corner of Breynat and McDougal and sat down on one of the benches there, watching the cars and pickups go past. It was not long after five and the brief homeward rush had begun. Ignoring the traffic, ravens strutted at the street's edges with a nervous arrogance, calling to one another from pavement to telegraph pole to cathedral roof. A breeze brought dust and cool air up the road, dragging the evening behind it. I stopped and listened a while longer, focusing my ears on the dull white noise that hung like a mist in the air. Beneath the urgent cawing of the ravens, and beneath the sounds of the street, was a thin whispering on which all the other noise was built. That whisper was the river.

At the beginning of the twentieth century, Fort Smith was still a very long way from civilisation. In western Canada, the Klondike gold rush had led to a massive influx of people. The Yukon Territory had been connected to the outside world by railway, by telegraph and by economics, but change had not come so quickly elsewhere, and trappers, traders and missionaries were still virtually the only non-native people living above sixty. Things were beginning to change, though, and the pace of development would quicken over the coming decades. Increasing quantities of food, trading goods and machinery were carried through the Fitzgerald-Smith corridor, particularly after the discovery of oil at Norman Wells in 1920, uranium at Port Radium in 1930 and gold at Yellowknife in 1934. The fortunes of Fort Smith were inextricably linked to those of the Territory itself, and when the American army arrived in town in the early 1940s, major changes were under way across the north.

During the Second World War, the United States took on two major building projects in Canada. The first was the Alaska Highway, passing through British Columbia and the Yukon, which the army completed with immense effort in just eight months in 1942. The road cut a 1,700 mile slice through a part of the country few had ever visited, and it made regular land access to the north a reality for the very first time. The second project was the Canol (Canadian Oil) road and pipeline, between Norman Wells and Whitehorse. Equipment and supplies for that project had to be carried through Fort Smith, and the increase in traffic required an upgrade of the portage road from Fort Fitzgerald, which the army undertook. The work also necessitated a winter road to Hay River, on the south shore of the Great Slave Lake. These projects, along with the air bases the army constructed at Smith and elsewhere, changed the north forever. The region would never again be so isolated from the rest of the country. When the Second World War came to an end, the population quickly began to rise.

Canada's north is woven together with the stories of people who've chosen to leave the south behind. A considerable percentage of the non-indigenous population were born elsewhere, and they bring with them a profusion of histories. Some come here to escape the frantic pace of the south; others come to find work, or quiet. Some stay only a short time; others never leave. But these people bring to the north an instinct towards change. They help to create a sense of a place not yet complete, a place still in the making.

One such immigrant is Ib Kristensen, who has spent more than forty years in Fort Smith. On a warm afternoon I sat with him outside North of 60 Books on Portage Avenue, the shop and café that he and his wife Lillian opened together in 1975. We sipped our coffees and watched as his sheepdog ran to greet each visitor to the store. A few ragged clouds moved overhead, throwing thin shadows onto the grass around us. Ib leaned back in his seat, his white hair and beard neatly trimmed, his glasses perched comfortably upon his face. He smiled as he spoke of the half-lifetime he'd spent in this town. 'I'm very fortunate to have found this place,' he told me.

In the winter of 1959, after a stormy Atlantic crossing, Ib and Lillian arrived in Halifax, Nova Scotia. They had $400 in their pockets and not a word of English in their mouths. Remembering how he felt on that cold day, more than fifty years ago, Ib shook his head. 'How on earth did we get here?' he laughed. Just a few months before, the couple had walked into a Canadian government travel bureau in Copenhagen and sat down to watch a film about Vancouver. They'd made up their minds to leave Europe, but hadn't yet decided where they would go. 'I didn't feel there was enough room for me in Denmark,' Ib explained. In that film they saw a place with more room than a person could ever need, more room than a person could even imagine. The pair signed their emigration papers that same afternoon.

From Halifax, the Kristensens travelled west by train through the vast belly of the country. They crossed from the Atlantic to the Pacific coast, arriving in Vancouver, which would be their home for the next eight years. Ib was a bookbinder and typographer, and Lillian a weaver, and both found employment in the city. But Ib's work would later take him back east, to McGill University in Montreal. There, the Kristensens and their two sons spent the end of the 1960s. But the stay was not an entirely happy one. Quebec nationalism was on the rise, and with it came an increasing military presence in the city. 'I grew up in the war,' said Ib. 'I didn't want to see a uniform ever again.' And so the couple looked north. They wanted a place where they could live together as a family and as part of a community, and in 1971 they chose Fort Smith. They purchased an old log house for $500 and the land it sat on for $1,000. Ib took a carpentry course at the college, and they made themselves a home.

By the time the Kristensens arrived here, Fort Smith had either become a victim of northern development or its beneficiary, depending on your view. Its former roles, as entryway and de facto capital of the Northwest Territories, had both come to an abrupt end during the 1960s. In the early years of the decade a road and railway had been built all the way from Edmonton to Hay River, bypassing Fort Smith and effectively making its portage route redundant. Then, in 1967, the Canadian government decided upon an official capital for the Territory, and 'luckily', as Ib puts it, 'Yellowknife got that'. While a few government jobs did and do remain, the focus shifted elsewhere, and the town's responsibilities disappeared. Almost overnight it changed from a bustling gateway to a place without purpose at the end of a long dirt road. Things could easily have ended, but they didn't.

Ib Kristensen is an old man now. He talks slowly, with the composure of someone who's considered his words long before he's spoken them. He smiles broadly and often, with a warmth that is both generous and genuine, and he talks of this town as though there were nowhere else he could be. There is a place for everyone, he told me, and this is his place.

When Lillian Kristensen died in 2004, Ib decided to retire and sell North of 60 Books. He joined me there as a fellow customer (albeit one who was welcomed with a hug by the current owner). As we sat speaking on the lawn, Ib recalled the freedom and potential he found here in the early '70s, when Fort Smith's future was uncertain. Those who shared this town felt a responsibility to create the kind of place they wanted to live in, the community was a thing to be moulded and improved. And that sense, of somewhere unfinished and bristling with possibility, has not yet faded away. 'There's an immense opportunity to do things in a place like this,' Ib said. 'If there's something you want to do and there isn't anyone else doing it here, you just start. If you want that kind of freedom, it's still here.'

When the portage route along the Slave River became redundant, everything changed. No longer was this town a key staging post on the road to the north; no longer was it held aloft on the tide of northern development. Instead, the country's eyes looked elsewhere: to Hay River and Yellowknife and Whitehorse. And the town turned too – away from the river, and away from the flow of people and money that had given it life. Fort Smith turned towards itself, and became, to borrow Wendell Berry's phrase, 'the centre of its own attention'. This was once a transient-hearted gathering of service providers on a portage route to the north. Like a commuter town, its focus was always on the elsewhere. But today this is not the case. Today Fort Smith is that most precious of things: a community that recognises and values itself as such. It has an inward gaze and a preoccupation with the local that both requires and reinforces a genuine acknowledgement of interdependence. That acknowledgement is crucial to the nature of the place.

We live in a time of great division and alienation, in which 'social networking', a parody of community, is passed off as a viable alternative or replacement for it. To recognise the interdependence of people upon each other – of people who share a place – is the fundamental act of community. And it is, today, a radical act, a willing and deliberate entanglement that ignores the siren cry of solitary freedom. The places where this is still the dominant way of living are, for me, places that foster hope. Not the hope that we may go backwards, and try to live as our grandparents lived. But rather, the hope that what has been diminished in this past century – the wisdom and intimacy of community life – may not be entirely lost. Fort Smith is such a place, and the reasons it remains so are primarily geographical.

Where economic factors allow, communities are strengthened by remoteness. In Shetland, small islands such as Fetlar, Out Skerries and Fair Isle have maintained a kind of togetherness even as they have battled depopulation, job losses and other threats. In part this is due to the inherent centeredness of islands, but it's also an issue of simple practicality. In places such as these, recognition of the community is not really optional. Any other way of living would be destructive. Remoteness exposes the vulnerability of a place, and it makes clear the absolute dependence of people upon each other.

Fort Smith too is an island, surrounded not by water but by an ocean of trees. And it is certainly remote. Hay River is the closest settlement of any size, and a 350-mile round trip is, happily, too far for commuting or for regular shopping excursions. With the exception of those few who fly back and forth to Yellowknife for well-paid jobs in the diamond mines, Fort Smith's citizens are largely contained in Fort Smith and in the neighbouring hamlets of Fort Fitzgerald and Salt River. The community that's developed here, for that reason, seems very much like that of a small island. People recognise that they are indebted to each other, and that such indebtedness is not a burden. There is, too, a kind of levelling that leaves few observable social divisions within the town, and the relationship between 'European' and indigenous Canadians is generally good. (The population here is mixed quite evenly. Around one third are Dene, a group of northern First Nations with languages in the Athabascan family; one third are Métis, aboriginal people of mixed European and First Nations descent; and one third are 'white'.) For those who choose to accept the constraints of geographical remoteness and to stay put, a connection necessarily develops with the *here*, and that connection can grow into a deeper, broader engagement. Such communities are never perfect, but they strive in the right direction.

*

It was early afternoon. The hot, sticky day thickened and grew heavy. A dark warning grumbled above the forest, and everything hung silent for a moment. There was a pause like a breath inhaled, then held, and the pressure rose as though from the ground itself. The air seemed to stiffen around us like a tourniquet. And then the storm opened. The first fat raindrops fell in a clatter, then a roar, punching the dust up from the street's edge. Then came the thunder, raging into the town. Rain descended in great, gasping sheets, punctured by lightning. The ditches, which earlier seemed needlessly deep, were full and overflowing in minutes. Everywhere was water.

I escaped into the Church of St Isodore, part of the Mission Historic Park, where buildings from the town's Catholic mission are being rebuilt or restored. The hammering rain increased, and soon it was coming through the roof and in the door. Hail stones erupted from a bulging black sky. The noise was enormous. I wandered around the room, taking my time with the interpretive signs, loitering, until the girl behind the desk invited me to play pool on the old table in the centre of the church. We shouted to each other across game after game, struggling to hear above the noise outside. It was more than two hours before the rain eased enough for me to venture back out to the street.

Later, when the storm had cleared, I walked out to the bluff overlooking the river. From the bench there I could see the Rapids of the Drowned, and the white specks of pelicans on the water. I let my eyes relax into the view, enjoying the distance. For most of my life I've lived in houses that looked out over the sea. In Fort Smith, hemmed in by trees, I felt half-blinded, and that spot offered the nearest I could find to a horizon. I imagined that water rushing on to the Arctic. Ahead of it whole oceans had gone, while Fort Smith stood watching. The Dene name for this area is Thebacha: 'beside the rapids'. The story of this place has been defined by the river.

That night I struggled back into my tent. My arms were red and lumpy, sunburnt and bitten; I looked like a victim of some hideous disease. But the insects had vanished, and the evening was chilly and quiet. The jack pines around the campsite whispered and scritched, as though they didn't want to be heard, and the sharp, sweet smell of them filled the air. The more nights I stayed in the tent, the more I was conscious of the ground beneath me. I had no sleeping mat, and though I'd not noticed for the first few nights, I was now aware of tree roots, twigs and pine cones spread out underneath my body. I could feel their shapes pressing into me.

The storm broke again around 11.30 p.m., just as the fading light forced me to give up reading. A few distant rumbles had become closer and more frequent, and all at once the tent was lit up. I counted the seconds. One, two, three, four . . . it was twelve seconds before another crack and long burst of thunder filled the air. A few spots of rain turned at once into a deluge, clawing wildly at the sides of the tent. I sat up and checked that everything was tight and able to keep me dry, then lay on my back and waited. Another flash. Eight seconds. And another. Five seconds.

Wood Buffalo National Park was on high alert because of the long period of dry weather. Lightning strikes could easily set off a forest fire. The previous morning the sky had been blue-grey with smoke from a blaze somewhere in the park. The helicopters were out and the watchtowers would be manned. The rain was a constant howl on the canvas, and I closed my eyes, trying to let the sound wash over me. Somehow, I slept.

I was woken at six a.m. by the light and the cold. It was close to freezing, and I was shivering hard. I dragged more clothes on and curled up, trying to find some warmth. Sleep arrived again then, stealing quietly into the tent, and a clear, bright morning followed close behind, without a hint of the night's violence.

*

'White people have lost their relationship with the land', François Paulette told me. 'They must have had it or they could not have survived for thousands of years. But now all people think about is money. All they have in their heads is money.'

He looked at me, unsmiling, then returned to his lunch. Paulette is a former chief of the Smith's Landing First Nation. He is an influential and respected Dene Suline elder, who today spends much of his time campaigning on land rights and the environment. When we met, he had just returned from Norway, where he'd been invited to speak to shareholders of Statoil, one of the companies exploiting the Athabasca tar sands in northern Alberta. His speech that day in Stavanger began: 'What you do with your money is your business. But when you begin to spend your money in my territory [in a way] that disrupts and destroys our way of life, our civilisation, then that becomes my business.'

Paulette is an imposing and intimidating figure – well over six feet tall, with long grey hair pulled back into a pony tail, and a thin moustache on his broad, rough-sculpted face. As he enters a room, attention instantly surrounds him. Everybody turns to greet him. He shakes hands, asks questions and remembers names, like a perfect statesman.

As we sat together in a near-empty restaurant one afternoon, François spoke slowly and with a heavy accent. He paused between sentences, sometimes for long periods. During these pauses, he was not waiting for me to respond or to fill the silence. Rather, he was talking at the appropriate pace. He was gathering, carefully, his thoughts.

'The Dene culture is entirely about our relationship with the land,' he told me. 'It is a spiritual relationship. It is emotional, mental and physical. The land is sacred, and there are protocols for everything. When I take a plant from the forest I must leave tobacco in thanks. When I am out on the river I must thank the river.'

This insistence on gratitude and propitiation is not unlike that of the Inuit in Greenland. It is a focus on reciprocity, and on the bond between people and place. For the Dene, the land is not a resource, it is a presence; it is not something separate from their community, it is integral to it. When François told me about a hydroelectric dam that developers hoped to build on the Slave River – an idea first raised in the late 1970s but still no closer to reality at the time of my visit – he was adamant. By restricting the flow of the Slave and flooding the land above (some of which is owned by the Dene) the dam would not only 'desecrate the river', it would 'desecrate our history'. 'It will not happen in my lifetime,' he told me.

It would be fair to say that Canada's indigenous people suffered less direct violence, historically, at the hands of European settlers than those of the United States. But that would not be saying much. Over the centuries, native people here were exploited, discriminated against and abused. Battles over land rights continue to this day, and the active suppression of native traditions and culture went on until the late twentieth century. From the 1870s, thousands of young indigenous people were forced to attend 'residential schools' – such as Breynat Hall in Fort Smith – whose principal aims were the Christianisation and assimilation of 'Indians' into mainstream society. Often, children were banned from speaking their own languages, and some had little or no contact with their families for months or even years. Many suffered physical and sexual abuse in these institutions, and sanitation levels were often appallingly low; at least 4,000 children died, mostly from diseases such as tuberculosis.

In 2008, twelve years after the closure of the last of the residential schools, the leaders of all of Canada's main political parties issued a public apology, as did representatives of the churches who had run them. A 'truth and reconciliation' commission was established to assess the enormous psychological and cultural damage done, and millions of pounds in compensation has been paid to those who attended. The legacy of the residential system is an appalling one. In their aim of separating native children from their communities, the schools were very successful; but they were far less so when it came to 'assimilation'. Graduates often found themselves unable to fit in, either back at home or elsewhere, and a wide range of social and psychological problems became commonplace: post-traumatic stress disorder, criminality, alcohol and drug abuse, depression.

Although what happened to young native Canadians has been described as 'cultural genocide', the residential schools did not succeed in eradicating the traditions of indigenous people. Those traditions survived. And they did so, in part, thanks to the tenacity and articulacy of campaigners like François Paulette, who have helped to bring the concerns of Canada's First Nations to the fore. But François's words troubled me. His verdict on 'white people' sounded like a judgement that could not be overturned; it was a sweeping, cultural indictment. And that was hardly surprising. The Dene's relationship with the land has evolved over countless generations, and is passed down through stories and protocols. But these are culturally exclusive, and the ways of thinking they engender cannot be recreated from the outside. The understanding of the Dene is, for the rest of us, largely inaccessible. So if François Paulette is right – if European cultures have entirely lost the traditions by which a relationship with the land is maintained, are we then destined to be estranged from our places? Can we never truly be at home?

An answer to these questions was offered to me by Jacques Van Pelt, whom I met, so I thought, to talk about pelicans. This stretch of the Slave River is the northernmost breeding ground of the American white pelican. Their nesting sites are concentrated on the rocky islands of Mountain Portage Rapids, but I had seen them in the air, soaring like ghosts above the town. There are few people who have spent as much time observing, recording and studying these birds as Jacques Van Pelt. But on the day I met him, Jacques wasn't much interested in talking about pelicans, at least not in the way I had expected. Instead, he wanted to talk about connections.

Jacques came to the north in 1959 and moved to Fort Smith the following year. He was employed to work across the northern territories on community development projects for the government. Later, he and his wife ran a tourism company, taking visitors on excursions down the river and out on the land. When we met for the first time, Jacques greeted me with a hug and called me 'Brother Malachy'. He moved laboriously, but his mind was quick. He talked with enthusiasm and excitement, though with no clear train of thought. Some of his words made me wince, reminiscent as they were of New Age platitudes. He referred to 'the communion of people and nature', and advised that '"I" must become "we"'.

Jacques spoke often of circles, of how indigenous people had built circular homes rather than straight-sided ones. They'd understood the significance of the shape, he said, and recognised its physical and metaphorical strengths. The sixtieth parallel excited him for the same reason; it connected people and places. My conversation with Jacques also seemed to turn in circles. During the hours I spent with him we returned again and again to his vision of nature's 'connectedness' and 'togetherness'. When he did speak about pelicans it was to try and explain to me what these birds had taught him. Over the past few decades, Jacques had spent innumerable hours observing the Slave River pelicans, counting them, getting to know them and warning others about the fragility of their population. He had walked and kayaked throughout the region, often for weeks at a time. He had brought visitors to see this place that he loved, and to share it with them. And though he could no longer do these things, though his back was bent and his joints stiff and sore, he still coursed with a kind of static energy and a relentless positivity. And the time he'd spent with the birds, his time on the river and in the forest, were somehow at the core of the person he'd become.

I was drawn to Jacques, to his openness and generosity, and to the joy that seemed to brim up inside of him as he spoke. But the cynic in me recoiled. As I listened, I found it

hard to hold on to his vision of the world. I felt I was grasp-
ing at water, clutching at something that was vivid and alive,
but which slipped through my hands as I tried to close them
around it. And yet I couldn't brush off his words. I couldn't
ignore the feeling that I had missed some fundamental point,
something truly important that I'd not been able, or perhaps
willing, to comprehend.

It was not until later that it struck me: behind the
spiritualised language, behind the platitudes and the positivity, Jacques' lesson was simple. What mattered was not
understanding, exactly. One could never, just by looking or
thinking harder, fully comprehend the connections between
your own body and the pelicans on the river, or the river
itself. The extent of those connections was beyond understanding. What was important, rather, was recognition.

In *A Sand County Almanac*, Aldo Leopold wrote of a
'land community', encompassing the entire biosphere of a
given place. This land community is not separate from, nor
exactly additional to the human community; both are part
of each other. What he described does not require any kind
of spiritual insight or enlightenment to see, merely a certain
awareness of reality. The food we eat is born of the earth
and is fed by the lives of other organisms, by the sun that
warms us and by the water that quenches our thirst. We are
joined in a myriad of ways to the world around us. These
relationships are matters of fact, and they exist at every level
from the atomic to the macroecological.

Jacques' vision of connectedness was an active recognition of the interdependence of things. It was, in a sense,
the most banal and commonplace of understandings, a
conscious acceptance of what ought to be obvious. And yet
today, like the very idea of community, that act of knowing
feels radical. What Jacques was advocating was a kind of
placefulness: an engagement with place that is united with
and strengthened by our engagement with people. No one

can disconnect themselves entirely from the world; we are all dependent, always. But if we fail to recognise and to consciously reassert these connections and this dependence, if we fail to build placefulness and community, then we risk being homeless. And that is no kind of freedom at all.

*

After the storm, Sam Stokell and Shawn Bell, housemates and journalists at the town's paper, took pity on me and invited me to camp in their basement, which was drier than my spot beneath the pines. They looked after me, and supplied me with good food and good company. Then, on my last day in Fort Smith, and with the clouds departed, they took me to see the river.

Inside the car, the radio demanded our attention. A story about North America's growing Prozac addiction rolled into a feature on cocaine and its impact on the short-term memory of slugs. Inside the car, Sam, Shawn and I listened, and were finally unable to suppress our laughter.

Outside, a trail of dust followed us along the gravel road out of town. We turned left on the track that leads east towards the river, drove a little further, then stopped and cut the engine. Quietness fell upon us and we emerged into a sharp heat, held immobile by the trees. A steep trail descended from the road, and together we clambered down through the forest, led onward by the sound of the water. At the bottom of the slope the track opened out at the riverbank, a sand and mud beach littered with dead trees and scattered wood of all sizes. Here the river was perhaps a quarter of a mile across, and a thick, soupy brown.

Together we walked upstream towards Mountain Portage Rapids, the clamour increasing with every step. At the lower end of the rapids we gathered wood – lifting and turning the smaller pieces, collecting those that were dry – and arranged them in a sheltered spot on the pink granite bank. Beside us was the constant rush of the water, bound for the north. Surging white, the river twisted in upon itself in eddies and whirlpools, piling up in unbreaking waves. It was a ceaseless, tumultuous motion that was both hypnotic and unnerving. I found it hard to look away.

Crouching over the wood pile we tried to light our fire. Sam and I held the matches close in among the bark and twigs, hoping they would catch. A flame. Some smoke. Then nothing. Again. After several attempts, the flakes of bark began to crackle and a gasp of light leapt among the sticks. We stood back and watched as it spread, and smoke lifted from the pile of wood, palling skyward. The fire raged into itself and we retreated, lying out in the sunshine, waiting for it to settle.

Once the flames had sunk a little, the three of us gathered around the blaze. We skewered hotdogs with flimsy green sticks twisted from the forest's edge and laid them out on an improvised grill, the smoke swirling up from the fire and into our eyes and lungs. As we coughed and choked, the meat cooked with varying degrees of failure, until eventually each of us had eaten enough to feel satisfied, and we abandoned our barbecue for the rocks up above.

Two young pelicans paddled close to shore, and out in the river, amid the rocks and rushing water, were many others. Most were settled on the granite islands where they breed; some were fishing, holding themselves steady in the tumbling river, dipping their heads beneath the surface. Above us were more, heavy-bellied like seaplanes, with great yellow bills thrust out in front. The wings, pure white at rest, showed a dark edge as they lifted themselves skyward. Enormous and unwieldy on land, in flight they become graceful, gliding in the warm air with the black of their wings blinking as they fly. In a few months these birds would travel south to rivers and lakes around the Gulf of Mexico, returning again the next spring. Always they know when to move and when to stop moving.

I thought of Ib then, and of Jacques, who had come to Fort Smith and stayed, and of Sam and Shawn, who were here temporarily, to work, and then to move on to somewhere else. How can we know, I wondered, when we have found our place in the world? How can we know when we ought to cease our wandering?

The sky was a cavernous blue, without clouds, and the breeze rising from the river was just enough to keep the mosquitoes at bay. A raven explored the fire's edge looking for scraps of sausage, its silent mouth gaping wide in the heat of the day. On the baking pink rocks beside the river, the three of us sprawled happily out and closed our eyes. The smell of the fire was in our nostrils and our heads were filled with the roar and hush of the rapids.

Shetland: Mousa Broch.

Greenland: drift ice near Nanortalik.

Canada: American white pelicans on the Slave River.

Alaska: salmon fishermen on the Kenai River.
(John Tobin Photography, www.tobinphoto.com)

St Petersburg: the Bronze Horseman.

Finland: the Old Town of Ekenäs.

Sweden: Gamla Uppsala.
(Erwin Spil, www.erwinspil.com)

Norway: Stolmen.
(Fihu, www.flickr.com/photos/fihu, licensed under CC BY-SA 2.0)

ALASKA
back to nature

The rain was not falling, exactly, but clinging to the air, as though in expectation of a fall. A haze of grey evening mizzle softened the street, washing all memory of warmth away. I sat alone, looking out through the window of a café, my fingers cradling a heavy caribou burger. I was the only customer. Outside, crowds of elderly men and women trudged up and down Fourth Avenue, wrapped in dark waterproofs, their hoods raised like congregations of monks all bowed against the unholy elements.

Seward's small-boat harbour was filling up with cruise ships and charter vessels, from which these sodden swarms were emerging. All along this part of the avenue were restaurants, souvenir shops and businesses flogging fishing and wildlife trips. Most of the buildings strove towards a kind of small town quaintness, but did not succeed. They seemed too desperate, too insistent, to be anything other than what they were: tourist bait.

The door opened and cold air poured through, shrinking the room. A gaggle of damp children and parents followed the draught in towards the counter, chattering to each other. I hauled my coat up around my shoulders and continued to chew at the thick slab of bread and meat in front of me.

All around Resurrection Bay, the mountains were swaddled in cloud, almost hidden and yet as present and as dominating as if they'd been standing among the shops and cafés. The mountains were the backdrop to everything here,

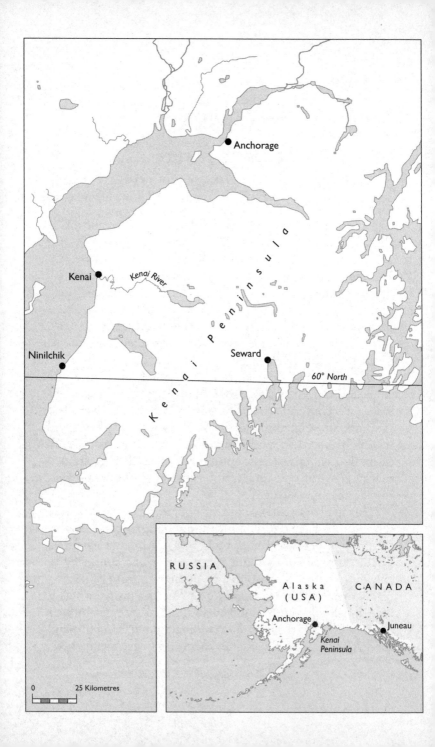

Anchorage

Kenai

Kenai River

Ninilchik

Kenai Peninsula

Seward

60° North

0   25 Kilometres

RUSSIA

Alaska
(USA)

CANADA

Anchorage

Juneau

Kenai
Peninsula

and I gazed out across the water at them, eager to ignore, for a moment, the foreground of noise and activity.

Seward is a tourist town, and offers its visitors plenty of ways to part with their money. There is, on its streets, that sense of hospitality polluted by retail, where smiles and warm greetings feel always like the foreplay to a sale. Yet despite the proliferation of souvenir stalls and nice-places-to-eat, and despite the affected charm of the old town, Seward's main selling point is not itself but its surroundings. On the east coast of Alaska's Kenai Peninsula, which lies south of Anchorage, the town is at the end of both the highway and the railway, and is a convenient platform from which to dip one's toes into 'the wilderness'. Both Kenai Fjords National Park and the Alaska Maritime National Wildlife Refuge are close by; forests, glaciers and fjords are all easily accessible. Like many other such towns, Seward has become what it is because of its proximity to what it is not.

Without doubt, the most effort-free way to experience these wild places is to be taken to them by boat. Day-trips and mini-cruises in the national park abound, each promising views of wildlife – sea otters, sea lions, whales – as well as lunch stops on remote beaches and empty islands, and a chance to see the Alaska that lies beyond the tarmac. Each morning, beneath heavy clouds, I watched the flotilla of tour boats pushing southwards through the bay, their onboard guides audible even from shore, the crackle of loudspeakers drifting over the still water. It was a strange sight, this armada, with its cargo of expectant tourists, eager to glimpse something that perhaps even they could not quite specify. For what was this thing that drew them out there? What was it that took them north in the first place? What exactly did they hope to find?

It is said that Vitus Bering, who was not quite the first European to reach Alaska, but who thought that he was and is widely remembered as such, was not impressed by what he saw. Suffering, perhaps, from the stifling melancholy of one who does not expect to see his home again, and from the unknown malaise that soon would kill him and prove his fears well-founded, the Dane looked upon this place 'indifferently and without particular pleasure'. This was his second voyage to the Russian far east, in the service of the imperial powers in St Petersburg, and in the summer of 1741 his ship, the *St Peter*, finally reached the North American continent. According to Georg Steller, the German naturalist on board, their captain did not rejoice at his discovery, but instead 'in our very midst shrugged his shoulders while gazing at the land'. The crew were fools, Bering declared, 'full of expectations like pregnant windbags!' They 'do not consider . . . how far we are from home, and what accidents may yet happen.'

The *St Peter* anchored on 20 July, near what is now called Kayak Island, in the Gulf of Alaska, five degrees east of Seward and only a couple of miles from the sixtieth parallel. Steller spent the few hours he was granted ashore breathlessly exploring the island, gathering new plant species and making notes on the native human inhabitants, half intoxicated by the delight of discovery.

Bering, in contrast, did not even bother to disembark. In this place that so thrilled and enthralled the scientist, the captain had little interest. Instead, he seemed haunted by the fear of what lay ahead, and anxious to escape before a possible change in the weather. On the morning after their arrival, before his crew had even had time to fully replenish the ship's fresh water supplies, Bering announced that they were to sail westward again for Kamchatka. Those who protested the decision were ignored, and the *St Peter* that day began its journey back to Russia. The captain, along with thirty of his seventy-six-strong crew, did not survive the crossing.

The land Bering found that summer was a place thus far untroubled by the careless hands of colonists, traders and professional adventurers. It was a place of immense forests and towering mountains; of fish-filled rivers and wing-beaten skies; of coastal waters crowded with sea otters, fur seals and whales; of plenitude and abundance; of a natural wealth that seemed, at first, boundless. And though like others after him Bering was unable to see it, Alaska was a place of dazzling, exhilarating potential.

The men and women who crowded onto these tour boats every morning, and who chugged out of the bay and then back again at night, were looking for what Steller saw. They were hunting for that place of abundance and boundlessness which greeted the very first arrivals in Alaska. They were trying, in some curious way, to go back in time. I found myself torn. I wanted to join one of these tours, to sail away from the town and see for myself the wildlife and the wilderness, and then to return to Seward in the evening, to a café meal and the relative comfort of my sleeping bag and tent. But something held me back, and for some days I struggled to reconcile my feelings. What troubled me most, I think, was the idea – advertised incessantly – that out there somewhere was the real Alaska, and what was here was something else, quite different. Those well-waterproofed tourists had been promised a journey into another world, and yet it seemed to me that that world was made impossible by their very presence within it. For what those passengers were being promised was their own absence, and that is something we can only imagine. Perhaps I was wrong, but I thought I could see disappointment in those faces as they disembarked and spread out among the town's restaurants and hotels in the evening.

On my final night in Seward I sat beside the shore, looking southwards across the bay, a cheese sandwich clutched in my hand. That afternoon, the sky had been a wide palette of greys, but the clouds were dispersing as the light diminished. I was close to moving on when I saw it, and when I did I almost laughed. Down in the water, just a few metres away, was a sea otter – pale-faced and as sleek as polished walnut. I watched it, amazed. I saw it dive, then resurface, oblivious to or unconcerned by my presence. It lay there, sprawled on its back, one foot then the other breaking the surface, then sinking again. The otter had caught what looked like a crab, and I could hear the crunch of its teeth against the shell. It clung on, sometimes knocked off balance by the swell, but each time rolling back into position, like a kayaker.

I sat for ten minutes or more and I could see, or thought I could see, the pleasure it found in its meal, the catlike satisfaction on its face. And when, moments later, a sea lion porpoised its way past the otter, I did laugh. I hadn't needed to leave town. The other world had found me.

*

'This is about as far from pristine Alaskan fishing as you can get', said Jeff, from the other side of the boat. I smiled back. 'That's okay,' I said, and nodded. And it was okay. Like many anglers, I had dreamed about coming to this place for so long that I wasn't going to let my enjoyment be dimmed by the fact that I wasn't there alone. I felt lucky, and perhaps even a little smug. I certainly did not feel disappointed.

The Kenai River runs from Kenai Lake in the centre of the peninsula to Cook Inlet, eighty miles to the west. It is a beautiful river – milky blue and sun splashed – and extremely popular with fishermen and seekers of white water. We had launched our boat (a 'cataraft', in fact: a metal frame held between two inflatable tubes, with a pair of seats on either side and another perched in the centre for the oarsman) at Cooper Landing, just below Kenai Lake, and were drifting downstream in search of fish. We shared the river with other anglers, in boats and on the shore, as well as with tour groups chasing rapids. In addition to these mostly quiet companions was the Sterling Highway, which ran alongside the upper stretch of the river. And though it may not be the busiest of roads, the hum of traffic was nevertheless a continuous accompaniment to the sighing of the water.

But fishing has a way of blocking out those things you wish to ignore; it has a way of disguising what needs to be hidden. The water around us swelled in our eyes and ears until it filled us, like a daydream or a vision. We were not alone, but we could just as well have been. Around us was forest, and beyond, snow-smeared slopes. Above the water, swallows danced like butterflies; and higher, a bald eagle cruised, as though following the same unquenchable current as the boat. All about us was the white noise of air and water, while beneath, the river flexed and writhed like a muscle.

We floated onward, our eyes wandering from the rod tips to the mountains around us. Slow drifts gave way to faster, shallower water, then deep, swirling pools. Mike, who held the oars, kept us as close to the 'good water' as he could, letting us know whenever he felt optimistic, or whenever we approached a likely spot. We cast, letting the heavy flies sink, then working them along the bottom, each retrieve imbued with hope and a renewed vision of the phantom trout below. Time and again we would approach those spots, those places of expectation. The water would move in the right way around the rocks; our eyes and fingers would focus on what could not be seen; every part of us would be ready for that moment when, as Ted Hughes wrote, 'the whole river hauls'. And then we were past. The boat would slip onwards and carry us away, and we would breathe comfortably again.

I have often thought that fishing brings a changed relationship with time. That mix of concentration and expectation, that sharpened gaze at float or fly, expands the present in every direction. Unlike the hill, in Shetland, where time contracts, out on the water it balloons. It admits more detail and swells, towards a prodigious breadth. Connected to an unseen world, the angler watches and waits with something more than patience. Lightheaded, both utterly present and absent at once, all attention is there, where air meets water. Vision and touch become entwined. Time extends, as it does in the moment of an accident, and eventually, as Norman Maclean wrote, 'all things merge into one'.

To fish is to be held in the heart of a stillness in which nothing is still. It is to wait patiently for a time that has already been imagined, yet which may never come. It is to live between tenses, in the anticipation of a perfect present. It is to be tangled in three time zones at once. As I fish – as I wait for the future to grab hold – I cannot help but be carried back to other days and other places. I am brought home, to cool, summer evenings in Shetland, where bright trout dash and tremor in black, peaty lochs. And further, to my first encounters with the water, in streams and ponds in Sussex, where I threw my cork floats and safety-pin hooks, hopeless but filled with hope. And then, again, to that warm, August day, when my father left me at the lakeside and never came back, when I lost so many things at once that I had never even dreamed of losing. All of this is held in the act of cast and retrieve, cast and retrieve.

Jeff and I first met in the early weeks of 2002. We were exchange students then, living for half a year in Copenhagen, studying at the city's university. We were taking Danish language lessons weekly, and one evening found ourselves sitting side by side in class. We did not immediately get along. Both of us were quiet, with a youthful inflexibility. We thought we understood things that neither of us truly did, and we had drawn our understandings from quite different directions. Our views, on politics in particular, were very far apart. On our first meeting I offended Jeff with an offhand comment about his country's president, and that could easily have been the end of it. We need never have spoken again. But we did – first out of politeness, and then from a mutual respect. Finally, we spoke for pleasure. Of all the people I met in that city, he is the only one with whom I am still in contact. We became friends, hesitantly, and we remained friends.

After university, Jeff moved to Alaska with his wife, who is from the state, and later they started a family. He had long dreamed of living in the north, and she wanted to come home. Since then, we had met only once, very briefly, in Shetland. So our friendship, by the time I visited, was concentrated in a time that had passed. The months we had spent together seemed a long distance away, and our communication in the intervening years had been brief and occasional, and in writing only. It had left an awkwardness, of which we both were aware, though neither mentioned it. But in the boat, connected to the water, that awkwardness drifted away. The space between past and present dissolved and faded into nothing. The river held us together.

There are many times in my life that I remember with longing. Some of them are clear to me now – I can see them, hear them, smell them – but they are never clear enough. I can hear the swishing of my father's corduroy trousers as we walked together; I can feel the pace and weight of his step. But I can no longer remember the sound of his voice. It is lost, and I cannot bring it back. Some nights I lie awake, gripped by a hollow, crushing nostalgia. Some days the desire to go backwards, to another time or place, is so strong that I am almost dazzled by tears. There are people whom I miss. There are places I have not seen in many months or years, but which are as plain to me now as if I left them only yesterday. They are as much a part of my present as the trees and the water, and the fish that I cannot see.

We look back, I think, towards times when we were not looking back. We are nostalgic for the absence of nostalgia. We long for those moments when we were not longing for what we could not have. We are restless to find rest. At home, beneath skies that I have known for most of my life, I still think of other places where I have lived – of Fair Isle and Prague and Copenhagen and Sussex – and I feel an aching, unquenchable homesickness. That feeling is related but not identical to the one that accompanied me through my teenage years. It is less hopeless, more inevitable. I think of all that cannot be brought back – a storm of pleasures, gone – and I curse my memories, just as I curse the lack of them.

Nostalgia was first recognised by Swiss doctors in the late seventeenth century. An illness primarily affecting soldiers at war, it was, literally, home-sickness, from the Greek *nósto*: to return home. For almost 200 years the disease – which was characterised not just by intense longing but also anxiety, lack of appetite, fainting, stomach pains and in the worst cases even death – was considered a serious physical ailment. The only cure for the most severely afflicted was to go back to that longed-for place. Yet this sickness is not exclusive to humans. Nostalgia is not our longing alone. It would be fair, indeed, to see homesickness as the crucial force that brings life to the Kenai, to Alaska, and to this whole corner of the continent. For what else, in truth, could you call that instinct – that desperate, anadromous urge – that pulls salmon back into this river, and to thousands of other rivers like it? What else could it be that brings those fish home, but an awesome and ultimately fatal nostalgia?

Around the 10th of June each year, the first sockeye or red salmon enter the Kenai from the sea. This particular run of fish are heading for a tributary called the Russian River. They are predictable both in their timing and their destination. Earlier, from the middle of May, the first king salmon, or chinook, climbed the river. Another run of kings will come in early July, and another of reds a few days later. In addition to these there will be two runs of coho or silver salmon – one in August, one in September – and finally, every second year, there will be pink salmon from late July through August. These fish are the lifeblood of the river. They are, indeed, the lifeblood of the whole Pacific Northwest. In extraordinary, incomprehensible numbers the salmon return to those places where they were born. In the same shallows and gravel beds from which they first emerged, thousands, then millions of fish come together to spawn. Then they will die. Great writhing masses of these creatures, increasingly grotesque as the end approaches – their skin discoloured and peeling, their flesh already rotting on the bone – will reach a place and then stop. This is their home, from where they can neither go on or go back. And by stopping there, by dying, they become in turn a part of the place itself. The flood of protein from their decaying bodies feeds everything, directly or indirectly, from the bears and eagles to the soil and the trees, and the next generation of salmon. It will feed, too, a great many people.

I had heard about the crowds that congregated on this river in summer and autumn. I had seen photographs too. But still I wasn't prepared for the sight that met us as we drifted down beneath the highway bridge and past the confluence of the Kenai and the Russian, where the sockeye fishermen were congregated. It was surreal and unsettling; like a carnival, at once horrifying and hilarious. A line of anglers filled the southern bank of the river, opposite the road. They stood perhaps two or three metres apart, like a picket fence, stretched as far as we could see. Along the bank only the occasional splash of a hooked salmon disturbed the remarkable, rhythmic order of it all.

Such is the quantity of fish moving through the river during these runs that even this extraordinary pressure from anglers is not sufficient to affect population levels. Enough salmon will pass through this barrier of people to maintain present numbers and ensure healthy runs in future years. And despite the United States' reputation for relaxed attitudes towards conservation and sustainability, populations here are well monitored and restrictions strongly enforced. Any notable fall in fish numbers would be followed by reduced catch limits. In this state at least, the notion of salmon as a shared resource, worthy of protection, is a powerful one.

The three of us floated through the middle of this strange gathering, then hauled the raft up on the north bank a little further downstream, where the crowds were not so dense. We found our own spots on a narrow branch of the river and began to cast, the water flowing in one direction, the fish in the other. Time resumed its little games. Everything moved. Nothing was still.

*

Two days later, and a few miles north of Seward, I stopped in a car park at the trailhead for Grayling Lake. There were no other vehicles there, but the highway was close behind and the town not far away. The sky was overcast and a light smirr thickened the air. Scanning the last few entries in the visitors' book I was disheartened. 'No fish.' 'No fish.' 'No fish.' I considered moving on and trying somewhere else, but the afternoon was already half complete and my enthusiasm was beginning to wane. Plus, it was grayling I was after, and if I was going to catch one anywhere it would be here. I signed my name, wrote down the date and time of my arrival (so that potential rescuers would have my details, should I go missing) and unpacked my things from the truck.

Stepping off the gravel and on to the trail, it seemed a line was crossed. Or perhaps it would be more accurate to say that some kind of balance was overturned. A car park in Alaska is not everyone's idea of civilisation, and a signposted trail might not qualify as wilderness. But there was a change – a shift from one side of that scale to the other – and I felt the change inside me as fear.

One of the marks of civilisation, perhaps, is the uncontested place of human beings at the top of the food chain. Where competitors have not been entirely wiped out, as in Britain, they have at least been heavily suppressed, or banished to reserves and shrinking pockets of wild land. But in Alaska it is people who live in pockets, towns and villages connected by thin ribbons of road. Despite the steady encroachment of industry, particularly oil and tourism, the vast bulk of the state is completely undeveloped. Even the Kenai Peninsula, which attracts large numbers of visitors, is dominated by a national park, a national forest, a 'state wilderness park', 'wilderness areas' and the Kenai National Wildlife Refuge, a two million acre protected region, established by Franklin Roosevelt in 1941. Step outside the town in Alaska – step off the road or away from the car park – and the rules of civilisation no longer apply.

As I took those first steps on the trail and into the forest, the fear rose quickly in my throat. Moving between thick, new-growth trees, with visibility down almost to zero, I could feel my heart beat harder. My fear was complicated and confusing, but as I walked the thump in my chest found its focus in one simple word: bear.

With fishing rod, tackle bag and waders in my hand, I felt clumsy and vulnerable, and I stopped almost immediately to rearrange my luggage. The pair of waders were flung over my shoulder together with the bag. In one hand I held the fishing rod, and in the other I gripped my fingers around a canister of bear spray just inside my jacket pocket. I checked that I could remove it easily and quickly; I set my index finger inside the looped safety catch; I focused my eyes and ears on the forest.

Pepper spray is pretty much the last resort when faced with a brown bear. Ineffective at a distance of more than a few metres, it is useful only when you are being charged. And if you are being charged by an animal that can be more than eight feet tall when standing, 600kg in weight, and which can run as fast as a horse, it is important that the spray is successful. If it's not, your only possible chance of escape is to play dead and hope the bear loses interest. If you're lucky it might paw you for a moment, perhaps breaking your limbs in the process. If you're not lucky, you won't have to pretend to be dead very long. In the few weeks I spent in Alaska, two people were mauled by brown bears. Neither attack was fatal, fortunately, but both left the victims – in one case a workman up north, in the other a cyclist in Anchorage – in hospital.

The best way to avoid such an attack, I was told – other than to remain indoors at all times – is to be noisy. Bears become angry when they're surprised or threatened, and as a rule they will stay away from people, given the opportunity. Many hikers wear a bell to alert animals to their approach; others simply shout or sing as they go. Somehow it feels odd to confront your fears in this way, to let the danger know you are coming. I wanted to sneak through the trees unnoticed as well as unscathed, but I followed the advice I had been given, and I tried to sing.

As the trail rose into old-growth forest, and the sound of the highway was lost behind me, I could feel the presence of the bear, like a ghost among the trees. The space was haunted by it, as was I. Beneath the canopy of leaves, a whole array of spirits seemed to dwell. Invisible insects clouded my face and birds moved unseen above; even the trees themselves were somehow not unmoved by my steps. The whole forest seemed aware, and held me with an attention that was mirrored in my own vigilance.

The singing didn't last for long. Somehow no words felt right, and the sound of my voice was alien and intrusive. My mouth became dry and useless, and I took instead to humming, both random tunes and familiar melodies – some of them ludicrously out of place, yet still strangely comforting.

I imagined myself from the outside: a man alone, walking fearfully through an Alaskan forest, laden with fishing tackle, humming 'Mr Tambourine Man' as loudly as he could manage. Surely a bear would be more likely to laugh than to attack.

After ten minutes or so of hiking, something made me pause and turn my head. I stood still and listened. My breath was loud and my heart thumping. But another sound, too, broke the forest's silence. A rhythmic pounding like feet or paws, running in my direction. I turned to where the noise came from, and looked out among the trees. It can have been a few seconds only between hearing the animal and seeing it coming towards me, but in that brief time I had imagined, in detail, what was to come. The beat of my pulse had fallen in time with the thud of the four approaching feet. The spray had been lifted from my pocket and gripped tightly around the top. I had steadied myself in anticipation and in regret. And then, there it was.

Had I been given a chance to identity this animal before it came into sight, I would have needed a great many tries before guessing correctly. A charging bear might well have been unlikely, but a big, bounding Labrador with its tongue hanging out seemed equally so. At that particular moment I was not capable of laughter, but if I had been I would have doubled up and fallen to my knees.

The dog had a name tag but no name, only a phone number scratched into one side of the metal label. I waited for it to leave, giving vague commands and gesturing back to where it had come from. But there was no one around and the dog stood looking at me, apparently urging me to go on. Having longed for a walking companion, I had accidentally found one, and so the pair of us turned and continued on the trail, he following, then running ahead, stopping every few metres to sniff at something – a tree or invisible marker at the trailside. Watching him run, then turn, then sniff, then listen, then run again, I realised just how illiterate I was in that place. The forest is filled with signs, but I couldn't read them. There was a language there, a complex vocabulary of which I was barely even conscious, and which I couldn't hope to understand or translate. Clutching the spray can in my hand and humming like a fool, I was helpless: as stupid as a bear in a bookshop.

People who encounter animals in the wild often talk about glimpsing a kind of intelligence, an innate wisdom, in the eyes that return their stare. But that story can be turned around; those eyes can be mirrors. For what we recognise in that strange gaze, I think, is our own stupidity. Faced with a creature that knows itself and its place so completely, that understands its own purpose and needs without the burden of doubt, we see in an instant just how ignorant we are. Both animal and human will be filled with questions during such an encounter, but only the animal will find satisfactory answers.

This is the root of my fear: this educated ignorance, this absence of understanding. Bombarded with information that I couldn't interpret, I felt anxious and overwhelmed. My eyes were of limited help in the shadows of the forest; my hearing is undeveloped and my nose almost useless. With such inadequate senses I was at risk, always, of being surprised. And as my new-found friend had proved, even a creature that wanted to get noticed could catch me unawares. What I had to rely on were my thoughts – which in a place such as that were more crippling than comforting – and my instincts.

Carl Jung believed that, in our contact with the natural world, it is our reliance on language that puts us most at a disadvantage. 'Man's advance towards the Logos was a great achievement,' he wrote, 'but he must pay for it with a loss of instinct and loss of reality.' The result of 'our submission to the tyranny of words' is that 'the conscious mind becomes more and more the victim of its own discriminating activity'. Faced with the unfamiliar, we struggle to understand. Our map through the world – language – can no longer guide us. Instead it creates a distance between ourselves and that which we observe, as well as that which observes us. Like the bright, sweet apple upon the Tree of Knowledge, word divides us from world. It is not Paradise that is lost, it is us. I felt fear, then, and I hated it. I hated it for everything it said about me. There in the forest a deep conflict emerged, between my desire to flee from human places and my desire – increasingly acute – to flee from that place. I was drawn in and repelled at once; I was fascinated and afraid. The wilderness was as much within me as I was within it.

Eventually the nameless dog and I reached the lake, which emerged from the forest like an afterthought, or a clarification of something previously said. It had taken much longer than I'd expected to reach the end of the trail – perhaps 35 minutes or more, though it was hard to keep track of time – but I was relieved to see the water, and relieved to be able to stop. There was a good breeze coming down the lake and rain was falling steadily, dimpling the surface. Trees crowded almost to the water's edge, and through the fog bruised clouds bumbled down from the mountains above. The air was like gauze, greyed by rain.

I set up the rod and tied on a small, dark fly, rubbing grease into its feathers to make it float. I had no particular idea what a grayling might like, but that one seemed worth a shot. I waded in up to my middle and began to cast, watching the fly as it perched on the water. I put to the back of my mind the list of dispiriting comments I'd read in the visitors' book. I persevered. After fifteen minutes or so, when the fly had begun to sink, there was a twitch on the line, then another twitch on the next cast. Then nothing. I stepped out and walked a few metres further up the bank, then cast again, moving back over the same water. The rain was steady, but I no longer noticed it. A cast. Another cast. Then a hesitation. The line tripped as I tried to retrieve. A stop. I pulled again. Once. Twice. On the second pull the line pulled back. I lifted the rod and there was the fish. It splashed against the surface, the silver back and tall dorsal fin appeared. My first ever grayling.

Twenty minutes later there was another stop. A tug. I retrieved again and the fish was on, bigger this time. It put up a stronger fight. The line shook, jerked and wrenched in staccato shivers. A jagging in the water, a burst to one side and a deeper pull. Then a splash that tore through the silence like a gunshot, and that beautiful, perfect dorsal fin in the air. I killed this one, then gutted it. I held the fish in my right hand and the knife in my left, slicing first across the neck, then drawing the blade up through the belly, pulling the insides out and letting them slip back into the water. I cut the head and tail off and dropped them, watched them sink, then wrapped the fish up and put it away. I washed my hands in the lake.

With that smell on my fingers and the fish in my bag I felt nervous again, and decided to go. I'd done what I came to do and was happy to leave the place behind. I packed my things away and arranged the waders over my shoulder so I could walk comfortably with the spray in my right hand, and I set off. Then I stopped. Just a few metres from where I'd been standing was something I'd not noticed before, something I didn't see when I first arrived. On the ground, almost hidden among thick bushes, was a kind of hollow, a space where the plants had all been flattened and crushed. Twigs were broken, and tufts of brown fur lay all around. There was an odd smell, too: thick and oily, like lanolin. Something had been lying here very recently.

In hindsight I wish I'd bent down to pick up a tuft of fur and bring it back with me, to be sure: was it a bear or was it a moose? But I didn't even think of it. Panic surged through me and I straightened, grabbed my things and went, without looking back. The dog with no name had long since abandoned me, and I walked to the car alone, wanting but not wanting to run, wishing for the trail to be over. It seemed to take hours, and that fear, that stupid, ignorant fear, never left me until I'd reached the car park and signed out. And there, in the visitor's book, I saw something else I had not noticed before. Three days earlier, someone had written the following words: 'Saw a large brown bear by the lake'. Had I seen those words when I first arrived I would never have set off. I am glad that I didn't see them.

That night, I took the fish from my bag, sliced the flesh, and rubbed salt and pepper into it. I fried it in butter, the skin crackling and tightening against the heat. Then I tasted the lake again.

*

I spent much of my time in Alaska driving. In an old red pickup I'd borrowed from Jeff, I roamed the Kenai Peninsula, following the highway from Anchorage to Seward to Homer and back again. With my rucksack, tent and sleeping bag piled up on the back seat, I felt a kind of freedom that pulled me onward down those winding roads. I followed mobile homes or 'recreational vehicles' (RVs) the size of coaches, overtaking no one. Once, on my brother's birthday, I drove nearly two hours out of my way in search of a payphone to call him, then drove back again, enjoying each of those extra miles. Mountains gathered around me like spectators, looming over the road. Here was a place where it was easy to feel small.

On a still evening, just outside the village of Moose Pass, I drove beside a roadside pool where, unconcerned by the traffic, a buck moose stood knee-deep in the water. He was enormous – two metres tall at the shoulders – and almost comical, like a cow on stilts. His strange, broad antlers seemed not majestic, like a stag, but fabulous nonetheless. Seated in that sealed-off little world, I rumbled around the peninsula, stopping when I felt like stopping. I would camp at night, though I never slept well. In those midsummer days, darkness didn't come, and I would doze on and off in the bright tent. Sometimes I would open my eyes, disorientated, unable to tell what time it might be, and only the silence from the road nearby would suggest that morning was still hours away.

The landscape was always astonishing. Sometimes it was hard to concentrate on the road, so beautiful was the world beyond the bitumen. Blue glacial rivers spilled through stony valleys, with white-capped peaks all around. Silvery lakes appeared, then were gone – rumours among the trees. Cottonwood seeds wisped through the air like flurries of summer snow. The sky folded and unfolded. The land invited both eye and mind. But all over the peninsula, among the pink and purple flowers at the roadside, among the trees and tall bushes, among the rivers, streams and lakes, there were signs: 'Private property', 'Keep out', 'No trespassing'. There were chains slung over driveways and roads; there were padlocks and high fences; there were lines that couldn't be crossed.

It's difficult to explain precisely why these signs offended me. Perhaps because I live in a country that does not have trespassing laws. Or perhaps because there is something about this place in particular, something about its vastness, its wildness and its wonder that makes the idea of property and of exclusion seem foreign. I thought back to Greenland, where land cannot be privately owned, and where the relationship between people and place is founded on the idea of use and of community. I thought of how appropriate that seemed, and of how inappropriate these signs felt. 'Keep out', they said. To which I responded, from inside the truck, with two equally offensive words.

In Alaska, as in the United States as a whole, the relationship between people and the land, particularly people and 'wilderness', is fraught with historical and cultural baggage. The land is a place to be exploited and to be preserved; it represents both the country's past and its future; it is fragile and it is dominating. Here too, the notion of a frontier, with all of that word's emotive implications, remains strong, and brings its own tight bundle of conflicts and contradictions. Not least over the issue of ownership.

Offensive though these signs appeared to me, private land ownership is in fact not the norm here, as it is elsewhere in the US. The vast majority of Alaskan land is owned, in one way or another, by the state or federal government, and the extent to which they allow development – whether it be large-scale mining or the building of cabins and homesteads – is understandably controversial. Less than one per cent of the state is in private hands, with an exception that, for outsiders, is surprising.

Native Alaskans did not own Alaska before Europeans arrived. They did not, in fact, know what land ownership meant (nor, for that matter, would they have understood the concept of 'wilderness'). They didn't need to. Like the Inuit of Greenland, the indigenous people of northern North America were users of the land and its resources. They dwelled and were at home upon it. Possession was not only meaningless, it would have been entirely counterproductive to a sustainable relationship with the place.

But that changed, as it did for native people across the continent, when the land they had never thought to own was usurped by colonisers. And, here at least, it changed again in 1971 with the passing of the Alaska Native Claims Settlement Act (ANCSA), under which the state's 60,000 indigenous people received one billion dollars compensation between them, as well as 44 million acres of land, split between regional and local 'corporations'. According to

John McPhee, 'This was perhaps the great, final, and retributive payment for all of American history's native claims – an attempt to extinguish something more than title . . . The natives of Alaska were suddenly, collectively rich.' This was in some senses a real victory, and it was certainly better than anything that native people had been offered elsewhere in the country. But the price of this deal was the acceptance of a system of ownership and of value that was not their own. It was, in other words, complicity.

Susan Kollin has written that 'the corporate model introduced by ANCSA has brought with it new forms of "institutionalized competition" between native peoples that had not existed before and that violate a standard belief in forging reciprocal relations with the natural world.' The effects of this change are social and psychological as much as they are financial. Writing about the enclosure of common land into private holdings in England in the late nineteenth century, Deborah Tall observed that, 'After enclosure, the communal sense of place and identity was divided into numerous fenced and hedged private loyalties.' Those private loyalties were imposed on native Alaskans under the terms of ANCSA.

Jeff recently bought a piece of land from the government. The state continues to sell off a few small parcels to individuals who wish to homestead or build cabins, and that is precisely what Jeff wants to do: to build a cabin where he and his family can spend time together, on the land. Doing so has been a dream of his since he was a child. Though he grew up in the south, in Washington State, he has always looked forward to this place, longed for it. When he finished university, this is where he came. And now, settled here with his wife and children, he makes sense to me in a way that I don't think he ever quite did before.

One afternoon, the two of us set out from Anchorage to visit his 'property'. It was a two and a half hour drive from the city, then a short way on a dirt track into the forest. When it became impassable, we got out and hiked, first along the track, then out into the bush. The going was slow, over fallen trees and brush, up a steep ridge to where the land levelled out, then began to fall again. A fire several years before had left some of the trees brittle and dead. Some still stood, leaning at peculiar angles, while others cracked underfoot. The ground was alive with plants – bluebells and Labrador tea. Snowshoe hares scampered behind bushes as we approached. Every few minutes, Jeff would call out, calmly: 'Hey bear, just passing through. No surprises here.' And each time he spoke I felt relief.

It was easy to lose direction among the trees, and we walked half an hour or so before seeing a lake out to our left. As we stopped to look over the water, I noticed the silence. No human noise whatsoever, just the air fussing among the branches. An eagle cried from somewhere not far away. Mosquitoes hummed around our faces. A stillness rose, as though from the ground itself. We found the corner post of the property and followed the ribbon markers around its edges, first towards a small pond, then out to another lake. Neither of these pieces of water is yet named, and Jeff is considering the possibilities before making his mark on the map. We had reached a place away from people, where things had no name. It felt a very long way indeed from the road, from the city, and from home.

I asked Jeff again about his motivation for building a cabin here, about whether he was trying to escape from other people. I could sense him becoming defensive. It is not about escape, he said, or about living some kind of outlaw lifestyle. 'I just want a bit of peace and quiet.' He knew I was uneasy about the idea of owning this place, and that uneasiness was tainting our conversation. But in truth, despite my reservations, I was deeply jealous. I was jealous of the comfort that he seemed to find here – a comfort that, in my fear, was not available to me. But if I am honest with myself, I was jealous too of the very ownership that caused me to flinch. It was a quiet, wonderful place, and I had no difficulty in seeing why he wants not just to spend time there, but to call it his own.

I felt guilty then for the suspicion with which I had treated his purchase of the land, and for allowing my dislike of that word – property – to become a judgement. Jeff does not view this place as a commodity. It belongs to him, legally, but his desire I think is for that belonging to become deeper, beyond law and title. What he hopes to find here, over time, is a kind of belonging that is complex and reciprocal: a relationship based on affection, devotion and love. I can understand that hope.

The two of us stood together beside the lake, looking out through a haze of mosquitoes. Three ducks cruised the opposite shore in silence. 'I like it,' Jeff said.

'I like it too,' I agreed.

Driving back to the city together that evening, we spoke with more ease and frankness, it seemed, than we ever had done before.

*

On the west coast of the Kenai Peninsula, the sixtieth parallel skirts the edge of a small town. Ninilchik is centred on the Sterling Highway but reaches out in both directions – down towards the beach, where the old village lies, and up into the river valley. Most businesses are huddled around the highway, seeking passing trade: the gas station; the wooden general store, stocked with knives, fishing gear and food; a Chinese restaurant; a diner.

Down at the long, stony beach, I sat beneath a warm sun. Streaks of high cloud were skeined over Cook Inlet, and on the horizon the hazy blue peaks of volcanoes loomed. Mount Redoubt, fifty miles away, towered above its neighbours, a scarf of cloud wrapped around its middle. A high wooded bluff hangs over the beach here, with cabins and campsites at its top. A crow patrolled the seaweed line, requesting, repeatedly, that I vacate his scavenging ground. Out in the water, salmon jumped close to the shore. Fish followed fish as the thick silver bodies leapt skyward, their tails flapping in the afternoon air, then returning to the ocean. At the river mouth, by the old Ninilchik village, I watched a juvenile bald eagle wade out into the shallow water, bathing. He dipped one wing, then another, then bowed his head into the stream, then lowered his tail. He splashed, stretched out both wings and shook, then repeated the process.

Down in the village, rotting boats and dilapidated shacks shared space with new homes and restored cabins. This is one of the oldest settlements on the peninsula, first inhabited in the early nineteenth century by employees of the Russian-American Company. When Russia sold Alaska to the USA in 1867, many of these workers remained, and overlooking the village sits a wooden church topped by five tiny onion domes. This is the Orthodox church, built in 1901 and still doing business, though services are in English these days. Inside, a three-part iconostasis is covered with gilt portraits, including one of St Herman, who came to Alaska from western Russia, then ended his days as a hermit on Spruce Island, in 1836. Outside, the cemetery was overgrown and blooming with life. An old man knelt among the white wooden crosses, mending the little fences around the graves and cutting dandelions away from their edges. Magpies hopped from the church roof onto the grass, then croaked back up into the trees. Eagles winged slowly through the blue above. Birds scattered their songs onto the ground.

People come to Alaska for many different reasons. In Ninilchik, they come to catch big fish. I met some of these visitors at the hostel where I stayed, overlooking the river. There was Bill, an octogenarian from Chicago, who twice a year comes north to fish or to hunt, and who sometimes brings his grandchildren. Bill likes to tell stories about his previous trips to whoever will listen. Then there was Frank and Elaine, from San Francisco. They were staying for two weeks, and every day he would pay for a charter fishing trip: halibut one day, king salmon the next. Elaine stayed behind, and when Frank returned she cut up his catch and put it in freezer bags, ready to take home. 'This fish costs us about $800 a pound,' she laughed. Frank looked at her and smiled, proudly.

Other people travel here to see 'wilderness', that vague, indefinable thing they feel is missing from their own lives. They come to experience nature, to gaze at it or move through it, and then to go home. There is a kind of nostalgia in this: a desire to return and to connect to something that is lost, or in the process of being lost. It's a longing for the country's past, for an imagined American Eden, pre-Columbus and pre-Bering. To visit the wilderness is to cross 'out of history and into a perpetual present', in Gary Snyder's words, 'a way of life attuned to the slower and steadier processes of nature'. That crossing, for some who come to live here, represents freedom. It is a chance to escape from rules and bureaucracy, and from the noise and muddle of the modern world. 'The last frontier', as this state is often called, is a kind of refuge or a spiritual haven, just as America itself was to the first pioneers, and it offers an opportunity for people to feel more like themselves.

Some people come to Alaska – and Jeff, I think, is one – because they dream of the place and that dream will not let them go.

*

On the shortest night of the year, I sat on Ninilchik beach, looking west. At midsummer, at every point on the parallel, the sun is above the horizon for just less than nineteen hours. And though it sets, it does so at such a shallow angle that the light never entirely fades. At worst, in poor weather, these nights could be called gloomy; but if the sky is clear it will remain light enough outside to read a book (or to play golf, as Shetland tourist literature is fond of pointing out). It is a strange kind of light, this midnight glow. At home it is called the 'simmer dim': a washed out blush, where colours fade and edges soften. Day melts seamlessly into day, and a connection is made.

At nine p.m., the sun was still high and a sword of light lay across Cook Inlet, resting its point upon the peak of Mount Redoubt. The mountains were paling into silhouettes then, with snow barely distinguishable from rock. They seemed to sit up, as though suspended just above the horizon, held aloft by a thin white line. Feather streaks of yellow cloud were ribboned through the blue sky. Just offshore, boats were still fishing, and through my binoculars I could see an otter floating on his back. A bald eagle was tormenting a raft of ducks, each one diving in panic as the raptor flew low above them, over and over. On the beach, four quad bikes hurtled noisily about, while a pair of eagles sat still at the wave-edge, attended by a squad of restless gulls.

By ten o'clock the sun was just over Mount Redoubt. The few clouds were backlit, glowing at their edges. A group of people further down the beach had built a campfire, and like me were waiting it out for midnight. I settled back and closed my eyes, with the wind against my face. I thought about where I was, where I'd been and where I was going. At that moment, I was halfway through my journey; I was halfway home.

By 11.30, the sun had slipped behind the mountains, and thick cloud was gathering over the land. The last dregs of the day washed over Cook Inlet, leaving only the sweet aftertaste of light. As midnight came, I picked up my bag and walked back towards the truck, leaving the night and the beach behind.

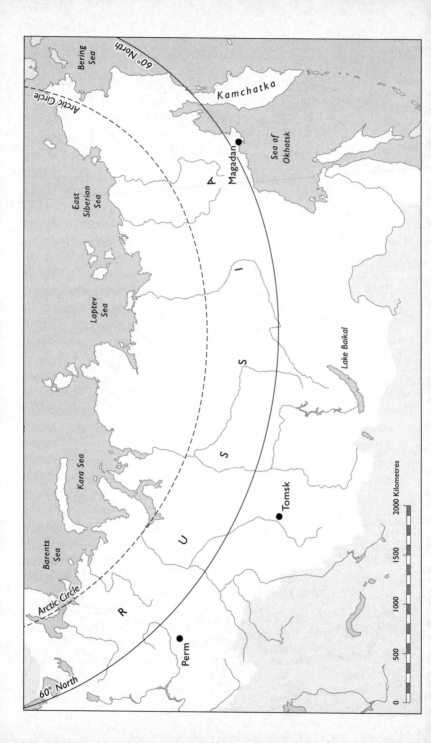

SIBERIA
exiled land

On a map of the world, there are few names that carry such a heavy burden as Siberia. Those four short syllables have come to signify more than just a place. They cast a shadow, and conjure a host of ugly images: of impenetrable forests and lawless towns, of poverty and alcoholism, of intense cold and intense cruelty. This is a region that lives in the mind, in daydream and in nightmare; it is more imagined than seen. And those imaginings, like a cloud of mirrors, reflect, disguise and distract from the land itself. This is a place almost lost behind its own myth.

To say anything at all about Siberia it is necessary to begin with size, for the enormity of the region is central to its story. Covering more than five million square miles – close to ten per cent of the world's landmass – Siberia has a population of less than forty million. It stretches from the Ural Mountains in the west to the Pacific Ocean in the east, and from the Mongolian steppes in the south to the frozen Arctic in the north. This is an area larger than the United States of America and Western Europe put together.

When I was twenty-one I went to Kamchatka, in the far east of Russia. I had found that wonderful name – Kamchatka – and a description in a travel brochure, and made up my mind to go. It was somewhere that nobody I knew had ever been before. It sounded exotic, and seemed, on the map at least, like a very long way away. Travelling there, from Shetland to London, from London to Moscow, from Moscow to Petropavlosk, it seemed even farther. That last part of the journey, between Russia's capital and its most remote region, left me struggling to comprehend the vastness of the country. The flight lasted nine hours and crossed eight time zones. The country passed beneath us, hour after hour, emerging from the clouds now and then but revealing nothing. Land, water, space, nothing. What lay below seemed almost blank, in the way that a desert or an ocean does. From that height, that distance, it felt empty.

Kamchatka, like many parts of Russia, was effectively closed to outsiders during the Cold War, even to most of the country's own citizens. There was, and still is, a nuclear submarine base on the peninsula, close to Petropavlosk, the region's capital, which was founded in 1740 by Vitus Bering, and named after his two ships, *St Peter* and *St Paul*. Kamchatka was also a base for international surveillance, being, as it is, one of the closest points to the west coast of America, and on hillsides amid the trees that past was still in evidence. But in the decade or so that had passed between the end of the Soviet Union and my own visit, doors had begun to open to the outside. Individual travellers were still discouraged, but organised visits were possible, so I joined a small-group tour company – half a dozen strangers in a strange land – and went east.

We spent just two weeks on the peninsula, but in that time I fell desperately in love. Together with my fellow travellers, I clambered into the stinking maw of Mutnovsky volcano and camped for two days beneath it, as the tail end of a typhoon stranded us inside our battered tents. I bathed in hot pools that sprang like blessings from the earth. I stood beside the Kamchatka River as Steller's sea eagles cruised overhead and a young brown bear patrolled the opposite bank. Dumbstruck, I looked out over land so vast and so beautiful that I could hardly believe it was allowed to exist. I left Russia infatuated. Something in that extraordinary place grabbed me by the heart and refused to let go.

For most of my life I have felt myself somewhat distanced from love – within sight, but just out of reach. It is a feeling that mirrors the sense of separation that was with me from my youth. And though it may partly be of my own creation – an avoidance of that which it would hurt to lose – it is difficult to be sure. These knots in which we tangle ourselves are not tied consciously or by design, we simply wake one day and find ourselves bound. But because of this distance, those moments in which love, or something like love, have taken hold in me have been memorable and important. And this was one.

*

The sixtieth parallel runs through the north of the Kamchatka peninsula, then across the Sea of Okhotsk to the 'mainland', passing close to the city of Magadan. That city, as much as any place in Siberia, has come to signify the horror for which, in the twentieth century, the region became known. For Magadan was the port and administrative centre of the Dalstroy organisation, which ran the gulags of the Russian northeast. These were the camps known collectively and infamously as Kolyma. The gulag system of forced labour camps, which reached its zenith under the watchful eye of Joseph Stalin, has come to be considered one of the most appalling acts of barbarism of the twentieth century. Many millions were incarcerated in these camps, and many millions died. The scale of what happened is almost as unimaginable as the scale of Siberia itself.

But the region's history as a place of exile and imprisonment did not begin with Stalin or Lenin, it goes back much further. Indeed, almost as soon as Russia started to explore the lands east of the Ural Mountains in the seventeenth century, Siberia's value as a dumping-ground for undesirables was recognised. In a twisted reflection of America's westward development, the movement of explorers, trappers and traders in Russia was accompanied by another movement: of people forced into exile. It is an extraordinary fact that, while the first European Russian did not reach the Pacific coast until 1639, by the end of that century ten per cent of Siberia's population was already made up of convicts.

In the United States, the West became a symbol of hope and progress for the nation; in Russia, the East was always a darker and more ambiguous vision. It offered wealth, in the form of furs and later gold, but it always remained a place apart, far from the heart of the country. While America expanded to fill its natural boundaries, Russian power and wealth remained where it had always been, on the other side of the Urals. Siberia was conquered but never fully absorbed into the nation. Such was the extent to which the region was viewed as distant and distinct, indeed, that when the Decembrist revolutionaries were sent into exile in 1826 for plotting to overthrow Tsar Nicholas I, one of their number, Nikolay Basargin, wrote that he no longer considered himself to be 'an inhabitant of this world'.

Those who were sent to Siberia were being punished for a wide range of crimes. From genuine revolutionary activities such as those of the Decembrists, to apparently harmless ones like snuff-taking and fortune-telling: all could result in relocation. And the precise form of that punishment also varied considerably. For some, exile meant little more than a forced change of address, but many others were sent to labour camps, the precursors of the gulags. These camps, like the gulags, had a dual purpose. They not only removed unwanted elements from society and placed them where they could cause no further trouble, they also provided a large, cheap workforce for the exploitation of Siberia's natural resources. These were not concentration camps in quite the same sense as those operated by the Nazis. Their purpose was to make money, and convicts essentially took the role of slaves. Death was not the intended outcome for prisoners. At least not at first. It was simply an occupational hazard.

While the tsars certainly made use of forced labour prior to the revolution, the scale and brutality of the system that developed through the early decades of the twentieth century was entirely unprecedented. In 1917 when the Bolsheviks took power, around 30,000 people were imprisoned in camps across Siberia. But by 1953, the year that Stalin died and the network began to be dismantled, there were close to 2.5 million prisoners in the gulags. This was a system of exile and slavery that riddled the country like a pox, and was fed in large part by one man's paranoia and thirst for vengeance.

Among the thousands of camps spread throughout the USSR, those in Kolyma gained a reputation as the worst. The region was, in Alexander Solzhenitsyn's words, 'the pole of cold and cruelty'. The isolation, the extreme temperatures, the difficult, dangerous work and the consequent high death rates became legendary. Prisoners were underfed and kept in unsanitary conditions, cramped together in freezing barracks that crawled with lice and other insects. In the years after 1937, when Dalstroy's first boss – considered too lenient by Stalin – was removed and executed, Kolyma was a hell from which death was the most likely escape.

To prisoners, Kolyma was known as 'the Planet'. Like Basargin a century earlier, those transported to Magadan felt themselves to be travelling towards another world entirely, and the sheer difficulty of reaching the place only underlined this feeling. To get there, convicts had to travel across the country by train, in overcrowded, filthy cattle trucks, with neither enough food nor water. In summer many died en route of thirst and disease; in winter they froze. The trip by train took a month or more to reach the Pacific coast from Moscow, and once there prisoners were kept in holding camps until being taken by ship to Magadan.

These ships, by all accounts, were worse than the overland transport. For much of the week-long journey, which took them through the Sea of Okhotsk, close to Japan, the convicts were locked in cargo areas that were never intended to hold passengers. So many were crowded below deck, some said, that it was impossible to lie down. Food was thrown into the hold from above, and the prisoners, often seasick and diseased, lived in their own filth. Common criminals ruled these 'floating dungeons', as the historian Robert Conquest called them, stealing food and clothing from the political prisoners and maiming or murdering anyone who got in their way. Women and young men were gang-raped, without consequence for the perpetrators, and those who died on the way were simply thrown by guards into the sea.

Such was the utter misery the journey entailed that the camps themselves may temporarily have seemed like a relief. Here at least was a ration of food for each person, and a little warmth, though not nearly enough of either. Here too was some modicum of order. Any relief would not have lasted long, however, as the reality of life in Kolyma sank in. The main job of the prisoners once they arrived at their designated camp was mining, principally for gold but also for other precious metals and, later, uranium. Prisoners were set work quotas that, even in twelve to sixteen hour shifts, were unachievable. If their productivity dropped too far, so too did their food ration. And if, as was almost inevitable, it continued to fall as starvation set in, they were likely to be shot as 'saboteurs'. The fact that there was not enough to go round ensured that everyone was always out for themselves. Gradually, reduced to little more than skeletons, ruled by hunger, thirst and exhaustion, the prisoners ceased to be themselves any longer; they became hollow people, with only the barest and basest of feelings. Varlam Shalamov, who spent fourteen years in Kolyma, wrote that: 'All human emotions – love, friendship, envy, concern for one's fellow man, compassion, longing for fame, honesty – had left us with the flesh that had melted from our bodies.'

Of those who survived the camps, many were broken forever. They were freed, but never free. In *The House of The Dead*, a fictionalised account of the four years he spent in Siberian exile in the 1850s, Fyodor Dostoyevsky wrote of how some convicts, once released, could not find the freedom they had longed for in the towns and villages to which they returned. Sometimes, 'a sedate precise man, who was promising to become a capable farmer and a good settled inhabitant [would] run away to the forest.' These former prisoners would become 'inveterate tramps', leaving behind their families to wander forever, living a life that was 'poor and terrible, but free and adventurous'.

Dostoyevsky's experience was mirrored in the twentieth century too, when some former gulags inmates found themselves unable to readjust to the settled life, to the towns or cities in which they had previously lived. Home, for these ex-prisoners, could no longer be located in a single place. Family, work, responsibility: all became chains that had, in the end, to be escaped. The taiga became home; the land itself was freedom.

Of course, Siberia already had its population of wanderers: native Russians – Evenki, Sakha, Nenet, Chuckchi, Koryak, Yukaghir and others – who, up until Soviet times, lived nomadic lives, herding reindeer and hunting wild animals. Their movement was governed by the natural migrations of the animals on which they relied. The idea of settlement – of tying oneself to a single place and staying put – was entirely alien; it made no sense at all in the context of their lives. To remain in one place in the taiga was to die.

In the region around Magadan, the predominant native culture was the Even, who lived in small family groups, herding reindeer. For 2,000 years or more, since these animals were first domesticated, the relationship between people and reindeer has been central to Even life, providing almost everything that was needed to survive. Their meat was eaten and their milk was drunk; their fur was used for clothing and for shelter; their antlers could be fashioned into tools. Fish, herbs, berries, wild mammals and birds all offered variety in people's diet, but reindeer gave stability. Without them, life in Siberia would have been virtually impossible.

Native Siberians' relationship with the land was one of absolute intimacy. In order to stay alive it was essential to know the places through which one moved, to know them psychically and geographically, but also to know their character. That character was the essence of the place, it was its soul or spirit. And for the Even, as for other Siberian peoples, spirits were a genuine, conscious presence in the land, to be respected, heeded, and appeased if necessary. Everything in this place had a spirit – every animal, every river, every mountain and valley – and according to Piers Vitebsky, 'Because such creatures, places, and objects have some kind of consciousness, they also have intention.' To live safely and successfully, therefore, one must 'strive to be aware of the moods of your surroundings and adjust your behaviour accordingly, in order to achieve your aims and avoid disaster.'

This understanding of the world, as a sentient place, would once have been almost universal. But it seems difficult to comprehend now when viewed from a distance, from the more or less soulless comfort of our own time and place. There are shadows of it still lurking, though, in our ways of thinking and in our language, and they lie not far beneath the surface. Siberia's climate, we might say, is *harsh*, and the land itself *cruel* or *unforgiving*. These adjectives are intended metaphorically, but it is not an enormous psychological leap, once we ascribe such characteristics to a place, to allow for the possibility that they might not be metaphors. To say that Siberia is an unforgiving place is to identify one element of its character, its spirit. And in difficult times, when faced by the reality of that lack of forgiveness, recognition of this spirit inevitably grows. In the *Kolyma Tales*, one gulag prisoner sees this with terrifying clarity. 'Nature in the north is not impersonal or indifferent,' he says, 'it is in conspiracy with those who sent us here.'

In central Kamchatka, my travelling companions and I visited a group of Even people. In the village of Esso, we boarded a decrepit orange helicopter that took us, noisily, nervously, to a treeless plateau that felt as far from our own lives, perhaps, as it was possible to go. As we stepped out and the engine was cut, the thundering of the blades was replaced by a thundering of hooves, as hundreds of reindeer – some white, some piebald, most a dark, chocolate brown – turned anticlockwise as one, in a tight defensive group. On the edge of the circle, men in khaki clothing stood watching the animals, one of them gripping a lasso in his fingers. Then, without warning, the loop was thrown and a reindeer was hauled out from the crowd. It emerged thrashing and dancing on the end of the rope – whole, vivid and vital. We watched in silence as the men dragged the deer away from the others, then pinned it hard against the ground. A blade was inserted in the back of its neck, just at the base of the skull, killing it instantly. What had been living and thrilling became dead.

It took only moments for the animal to be cut into useful pieces. First, slices were made up the length of the legs and the skin pulled back. The head was removed and placed upside down, facing away from the camp. Then, with breathtaking ease, the skin was stripped away from the body, and the innards removed from the carcass. More people appeared, wielding knives, with jobs to do. Six men and one woman worked together, cutting the animal into its constituent parts, disassembling it into food and fur. Cigarettes hung from their mouths as they bent over the body, cutting and dividing. A small, smoky fire was lit on the ground beside the meat to keep insects away.

When the work was done we were invited into the communal tent, a large, wood-framed structure, with an open fire in the centre and a blackened pot hanging over the flames. Into this pot, the deer's heart and other chunks of meat were dropped, and for an hour or two we sat together with the Even, speaking, drinking tea, and eating the animal we had just watched die.

More than any other event in the time I spent in Kamchatka, I have thought back to that day with the Even. There among the mountains and the reindeer was something that struck me and stayed with me, but which I have never fully understood. I knew, of course, that there is a falseness to any such interaction between native people and tourists, and that a deep economic perversity had made our encounter possible in the first place. But beyond that, beyond all of that, there was something else, something that moved me and which moves me even now. It was something in the thundering of those hooves, and in the parting of skin from flesh. It was something in the sharing of food. On that day I witnessed a familiarity between people and place that was far beyond what words could express. It was a bond that was more than a bond; it was a love that was more than a love. There in Kamchatka, those people were not really separable from that place. They and it were part of each other. It was a kind of union that once was normal and now is extraordinary, and though I knew that such concordance is no longer truly possible in the world in which I live, in seeing it I felt for the first time its absence. And from there, from that recognition, my own longing took shape.

That visit to the Even camp was in some ways misleading. While the life we saw out on the land looked much as we imagined it could have looked for centuries, in fact a very great deal has changed for all native Siberians over the past hundred years or so. Indeed, over that time, their culture and their way of life has been degraded, threatened and deliberately perverted, with consequences that are still being played out across the country. For the Soviets who took power in the early twentieth century, nomads were a problem. The native people's lifestyle, the authorities believed, was socially backward and incompatible with the new economy. Their solution to this problem was utterly destructive. From the 1920s onward, reindeer herding began to be treated in much the same way as any other form of agriculture, and was eventually brought under the control of enormous state farms. Herders became labourers, no longer working for themselves but instead for a wage from the farm managers. Animals became the property of the state. In addition, the authorities created 'native villages', in which herders were expected to live when not on 'shift' on the land. The number of men directly involved in working with the reindeer was limited – wages would be paid only to essential employees – and the number of women was limited much further, usually to just one for each herd. In this way, families began to be broken up, with fathers absent for long periods. The situation was made much worse by the removal of many children, who were sent to schools elsewhere in order to educate them out of their parents' way of life.

As well as these physical changes, the spiritual world of the people was threatened too. Shamans in particular, who had been crucial in perpetuating the native understanding of the land and its spirits, were persecuted, murdered and ultimately wiped out (the word 'shaman' is Even in origin, but similar figures existed across Siberia and northern Scandinavia, and still do in other hunting and nomadic cultures worldwide). The Soviets went to great lengths to try and replace native ways of thinking with their own brutal logic. In one example, shamans, who in their traditional rituals would embark on 'soul journeys' in which they would 'fly', sometimes held aloft on the back of a reindeer, were thrown out of helicopters to prove they could do no such thing.

The Soviets' plan, to a great extent, was successful, achieving much of what it was supposed to achieve. Though spiritual beliefs are still widespread among native people, the shamans have gone, and nomadism as a way of life was minimised as far as was realistically possible. But a high price for this success was paid by those who had to live with the impact.

When the Soviet Union collapsed, the people of Siberia were vulnerable in a way they had never been before. During seventy years of social upheaval, enforced from the outside, the communities of the region had lost the self-sufficiency that was once necessary for their survival. Reindeer herders who for millennia had been reliant only upon their own skills and knowledge of the land and its animals had become dependent upon supplies and services brought from elsewhere: upon vets, upon air transport, upon endless bureaucracy, upon vodka. And when communism disappeared, the economic safety net of the state disappeared, too.

In native villages today, the results of that change are all too apparent. Alcoholism, substance abuse, violence and suicide: it is a familiar list. Young people feel alienated from their culture and from their place. Women particularly, for decades urged to take up occupations rather than involve themselves in herding, now feel themselves entirely separate from that lifestyle. They are lost in a land to which they no longer feel connected.

What took place in Siberia – the enforced ending of shamanism, the restructuring and settling of native life – was an imposition of alien values upon a landscape and a way of living that was tied to that landscape. The Even's entire system of knowledge, their culture and identity, was centred around the taiga and around their reindeer. But during the

Soviet era, the centre became elsewhere. It moved to the villages and to the cities. The herders found that their lives had become peripheral. The taiga was now to be seen as a workplace; the reindeer, a product. At the same time that Soviet authorities were physically exiling prisoners in the gulag, they were psychologically exiling native Siberians from their own home, dividing them from the ways of living and thinking that had evolved in this place, naturally, necessarily, over thousands of years.

*

The longing for home and the longing for love are so alike as to be almost inseparable. The desire to be held by a person, or by a place, and to be needed; the urge to belong to something, and for one's longing to be reciprocated; the need for intimacy. These needs, these urges, these desires were within me when I travelled to Kamchatka, as they had been for years previously. But they had not yet found a way to express themselves. When I fell in love I had found something, somewhere, onto which I could project my longing from a safe distance. Kamchatka was beautiful and mysterious, and there was a stillness at its heart that seemed to calm, temporarily, the restlessness in my own. But Kamchatka was also, quite literally, at the other side of the world. By this time I had come to accept Shetland as my home, but I had not yet come to love it as that. The infatuation that I developed was a sign, first of all, that these feelings were building within me. And it was a sign, too, that place and landscape could be the foundation upon which love grew.

In the months that followed my visit to Kamchatka, I thought about it often. I kept in touch with people I had met there. I read everything I could find to read about it. I looked over my photographs obsessively. I even learned the Cyrillic alphabet and began to grapple with the Russian language. I made plans to go back, to spend more time there and, if possible, to come to know it properly. But I never did go back. Like all infatuations, this one began to fade. It ceased to occupy my thoughts to such an overwhelming degree, and it ceased, in the end, to lure me away. It was too expensive to go, I concluded, too complicated, too far away, and the reality of return was too liable to disappoint. Slowly, my dreams of Kamchatka were set aside.

*

As a place of exile, Siberia was extraordinarily effective. It is huge, cold and utterly strange: a natural repository for our fears and an ideal place in which to dump unwanted people. But the reason it has remained a land apart – unlike America's West, which was absorbed into the country – is, I think, as much about us as it is about the place itself. For in Siberia, the land and the climate resist the European understanding of home; they resist our desire to be settled. Pioneers in America did not move for the sake of moving. They migrated westward to find new places to live and to find land that could feed families and communities. They went to make better lives and to settle down. In most of Siberia, however, settling is an entirely unnatural thing to do. Much of the land cannot support meaningful agriculture, so towns and cities are reliant, always, on food and supplies imported from elsewhere. To try and settle therefore, means accepting peripherality. It is a literal and a psychological dependence on other places. Today, that is how the vast majority of the region's inhabitants live, but it remains a precarious kind of existence, vulnerable always to the impact of decisions made far away.

The appalling history of Siberia cannot be shaken off. It clings to the land, distorting and concealing it beneath the horror of what happened here. But the dark spirits that seem to haunt this region do not belong to it; they are not the spirits of the place itself but, rather, our own demons.

Western civilisation demands settlement. That is the relationship that our culture desires. But in Siberia, we are faced with somewhere in which such a relationship does not make sense. The native people of this region were nomadic because that is what the place and the climate demand. Their home was not a single location, it was the land itself, and their connection to that land – forged through hunting and herding – was entirely unlike our own. Siberia is an ideal place in which to exile Europeans because it is a place that rejects the European idea of what a home actually is. In Siberia, settlement itself is a kind of exile.

When I look back now upon the time I spent in Kamchatka, I can still recall those pangs I felt, and the deep longing I had to return. That longing was an urge to connect and to immerse myself in a place. I look back now upon Kamchatka with fondness and with nostalgia, as one might a teenage sweetheart, many years estranged. Sometimes my dreams of it return, and I wonder if I will ever see that place again.

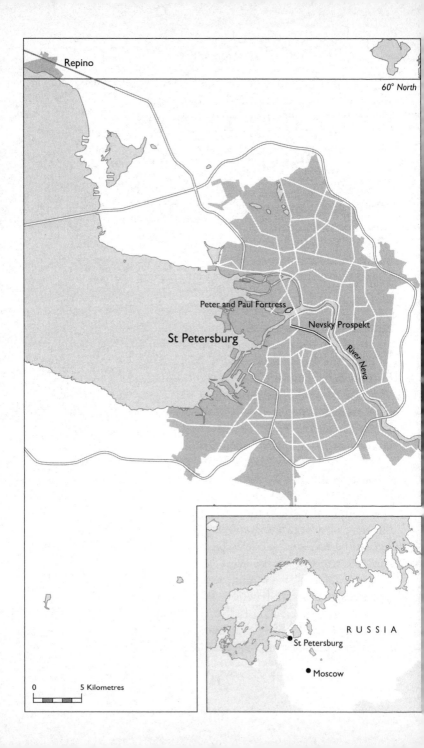

ST PETERSBURG
the city and the swamp

St Petersburg is a miracle city, which really ought not to exist. For three centuries, since its foundations were laid in swampy soil close to the mouth of the River Neva, both natural and human forces have conspired to try and destroy it, and several times they have almost succeeded. To many, it was a city that was doomed from the start. Its construction was an act of imperial folly that was bound to be repaid by failure. It was a place that did not belong where it was built, an affront to the natural order and to the nation itself.

Peter the Great conceived it while travelling in Western Europe at the end of the seventeenth century. There, he was impressed with London and most particularly with Amsterdam, and he imagined for himself a new Russian capital. When the long-disputed Neva estuary was won back from Sweden in 1703, Peter understood its importance. Up until that time the area had been thinly populated marshland, but it was also the only access that Russia had to the Baltic, and that made it essential for the country's development: culturally, militarily and economically. In the summer of that year, the new city began to take shape with remarkable haste. According to Peter, this was to be a Paradise on Earth, and Russia's 'window on the West'.

From its very beginning, though, the city was plagued by forecasts of its destruction. In its early years one prophet warned of how God would 'drown the Anti-Christ's city', and Peter's own first wife Eudoxia, whom he banished to a convent, cursed the place and declared that it would one day stand empty. Those predictions have sometimes seemed close to coming true. Great floods have swept through its streets, and fires have raged through its buildings. Devastation has always felt possible. In the Second World War, Adolf Hitler declared that he would be the one to finally destroy this city and empty it entirely of people, and during the 900-day siege of 1941 to 1944 he almost succeeded. More than a million died in those years, killed by starvation and by disease in one of the war's most appalling acts, a prolonged and deliberate mass murder.

And though he granted Leningrad – as it was then called – the country's highest award of honour in the last year of the war, Joseph Stalin was no more a friend of the city than his German adversary. According to the composer Shostakovich, Hitler merely 'finished off' the work that Stalin began. The Soviets had moved the country's capital back to Moscow after taking power in 1917, two hundred years after Peter the Great had done the opposite. They then set about emptying the city of the power and wealth it had hitherto accumulated. In the Great Purge of the 1930s, Leningrad suffered enormously. From ordinary families right up to Sergei Kirov, the Communist Party's leader in the city, tens of thousands of residents were exiled or executed. For Stalin, the city was a reminder of the old, tsarist Petersburg, and a symbol of the openness and cosmopolitanism that he so despised. It was, in Nikolai Gogol's words, 'a foreigner in [its] own fatherland', and after the war Stalin set about crushing it all over again. Those who had led Leningrad through the siege were murdered; writers, artists and intellectuals were disposed of in the gulags. The city's suffering continued.

*

It was a week into September when I arrived in St Petersburg, but autumn had not yet caught hold in this corner of the north. A warm wind bustled down Nevsky Prospekt as I pushed my way through the crowds towards the river. And though it had passed six in the evening the sun was still bright, lingering like a blush against the pink walls of the Stroganov Palace. From edge to edge, the wide pavements were filled with people: tourists in raincoats and baseball caps, striding businessmen in suits and shades, girls in short skirts locked arm in arm, old women whose headscarves could barely contain their peroxide perms. The street over-flowed with beeping horns and screeching tyres, over-revved engines, sirens and shouts; the smell of drains and exhaust fumes thickened the air. It was loud and chaotic, a heaving pandemonium, and I kept close to the buildings, nervous of the hustle and din that seethed between them.

Crossing the sluggish grey Neva to Vasilevsky Island, I lingered beside the red Rostral Columns that tower there, with their four marble figures representing the great rivers of Russia. Once, these columns served as oil-blazing light-houses, aiding vessels, but today their only role is to lift your eyes up and away from the filthy water below. From there I continued to Petrogradskaya and across the walkway to Hare Island, and the fortress where this city was founded. The Cathedral of Saint Peter and Paul shone butter gold in the evening sun, its gilded needle spire reaching 400 feet upward, to where hooded crows blinked like black stars against the sky. A syrupy light lay dappled among the trees around the fortress, and yellow leaves were just beginning to fall, a step ahead of the weather. In drains and on paths they were piled, dry and crackling underfoot. I kicked them as I wandered through Aleksandrovskiy Park, feeling a childish pleasure in that most irresistible of acts.

There is nowhere else like this in the north. By a wide margin St Petersburg is the most highly populated place on or above the sixtieth parallel, with five million people now living in the city itself and many more in the surrounding area. In that sense, as in others, it is an anomaly: a strange city in a strange place, a new city designed to look like an old one, a former national capital that was intended, from the start, to appear foreign. I had arrived on the twentieth anniversary of the city's most recent name change, when Leningrad became St Petersburg for the second time in its life. For nearly seventy years it had held the name of the former leader, a tribute bestowed in January 1924, just five days after his death. Prior to that, though for only a decade, this had been Petrograd – a Russification of its original, Dutch name, pushed through in the patriotic fervour of the First World War. For the two centuries before 1914, it was St Petersburg. But by most of its inhabitants it is known simply as 'Piter'.

It has been said often that St Petersburg looks like nowhere else in Europe because it looks like everywhere else, and there is certainly truth in that. Peter and later leaders employed architects from across the continent to bring their own styles to the new Russian capital. The only place that its founder was adamant it should not emulate was Moscow. Over the following centuries, as the whims of tsars and tsaritsas were made solid across the city, Petersburg took on a schizophrenic, pieced-together feel. It was beautiful, yes, but also haphazard. Neo-Classical palaces stand alongside Baroque churches, flanked by apartment blocks and mansions in what Russians call Style Moderne, or Art Nouveau. The effect is intoxicating and confusing at once. The only consistent feature is grandeur. This does not feel like a city that grew and evolved here naturally, over time. It feels like an imposition, like a city commanded into being – which is precisely what it is.

The next day, autumn awoke with a start. Dark clouds smeared the sky and rain shimmered along Nevsky Prospekt. Looking down from my room, high above the street, a parade of umbrellas scurried back and forth like swarms of multicoloured beetles, and I gazed half-hypnotised at the city below. The whole world was in a hurry, and everyone, it seemed, needed to be elsewhere.

A little later, sitting in a café downstairs with my breakfast, I watched them go by, hunched and huddled against the rain. I had no umbrella myself and no particular desire to get wet, and so I waited, sipping my coffee, then washing it down with apple cake. From the rooftops outside, enormous metal drainpipes were slung like elephants' trunks, water gushing onto the pavement below. In the street, trams and trolleybuses rattled past on their wires and rails. Cars fizzed over the wet tarmac. Everything on Nevsky Prospekt was moving.

This street is the most famous thoroughfare in the country. It was also one of the city's first, begun in 1712. It runs more or less west to east, beginning at the Admiralty building on the banks of the Neva and running three miles towards Uprising Square. Some of Petersburg's most distinctive buildings lie along this street: the Cathedral of Our Lady of Kazan, with its sweeping arc of Corinthian columns; the sprawling arcade of Gostiny Dvor; the Stroganov Palace, built in 1753. Here, as elsewhere in the city, an extraordinary array of colours can be found, some earthy, some rich, some garish. The stone buildings are painted lime sorbet green, pastel blue, sweet salmon pink, the yellow of fallen birch leaves. There are colours here that I have seen nowhere else before or since.

Over the past two decades, the commercial accoutrements of every other large street in northern Europe have arrived on Nevsky Prospekt and made it home. Designer shops, identikit cafés, sushi bars and expensive restaurants all jostle for attention. Window displays compete to draw customers in from outside. It is hard to imagine now, amid all this human noise and commotion, that for a long time the city's rulers struggled to wrestle this place from the wilderness out of which it had grown. Right through to the mid-eighteenth century, deer and wild boar were hunted around Nevsky Prospekt (then known as the Great Perspective Road) and the last reported wolf attack on a person was as late as 1819.

When the rain subsided later that morning, I set off to wander the city's streets. And for days on end I did the same thing: breakfasted and then walked, usually without route or destination in mind. When it was damp I went inside, to museums or galleries, or I travelled the metro from station to station. I took a boat trip though the canals to see things from another angle, and several times I stood inside churches and cathedrals – places of incense and gold and genuflection – where bowls brimmed with donated coins, and where, on one occasion, the glorious sound of a choir hung above the congregation's bowed heads like the proof of a better world to come.

On a day when the drizzle would not lift, I wandered until evening through the Hermitage Museum, overwhelmed by the rooms themselves as much as by the artworks they contained. The high ceilings were adorned with frescoes, gilded cornicing and enormous chandeliers of crystal and gold. There were walls of deep forest green and crimson, pillars of marble and of malachite, shining parquet floors. It seemed almost obscene, this concentration of wealth and splendour. There was something surreal about it all, something too perfect and controlled to be true. I felt awed and uneasy as I passed, room by room, through the Winter Palace. Such beauty, such luxury, such order. This city is truly the opposite of the swamp on which it stands. Which of course was Peter's intention all along.

On other days, without a watch or a phone with which to tell the time, I walked for hours, until my legs and back were sore, enjoying the absence of a schedule. I stopped to eat when I was hungry, or to rest my feet in a café, and sometimes I learned the hour by checking my receipt. But mostly I didn't even look. Joseph Brodsky wrote of St Petersburg that, 'There is something in the granular texture of the granite pavement next to the constantly flowing, departing water that instils in one's soles an almost sensual desire for walking.' I felt that desire and I kept going, returning to my little room only when it was dark. And as I lay down and tried to sleep at night, the city went on living and breathing, shouting itself hoarse outside my window.

As the days passed, I began to find new routes through the city. Ducking off the main streets, through gates and under archways, I found myself in what felt like other worlds – spaces quite apart from the commotion outside. Many of the residential buildings here were created with courtyards in the centre, where stables and servants' quarters would once have been. Some of these spaces are small and claustrophobic, others are light and open. Virtually all are accessible from both sides, offering an endlessly diverse means of crossing from street to street. On stepping in to these courtyards, the sound of traffic is immediately softened, and sometimes, when one yard leads through narrow passageways into second and third yards, something close to silence can be found.

At first I explored cautiously, like a trespasser. But as the days passed I found myself seeking out these places. This was a secret world, to which visitors were not invited. Here, cats padded through the shadows, and old men stood chatting with their neighbours. Sometimes there would be columns of ivy covering the walls, or a solitary tree reaching up towards a square of grey sky. Here and there were cafés and guest houses, sometimes shops and small businesses. In one cramped yard I found an umbrella-repair workshop housed in a ground-floor flat, with a tiny window for customers to knock. Once these areas would have been rundown and dirty, and a few still are. They were the secret, squalid heart of the city. But today the seclusion and quiet they offer is, to many, as attractive as the coloured facades behind which they hide.

From high above, on the colonnade of St Isaac's Cathedral, you can see the true extent of these courtyards. They stretch across the city like a vast labyrinth of calm, secreted among the buildings. A huge swathe of St Petersburg is concealed like this, off the streets and off the map.

Above ground, there are the courtyards; below, the tunnels and stations of the metro. Down there, in rattling carriages, I saw lovers kissing, old women laughing, and young boys in military uniform, accompanied by their mothers. The stations, built deep beneath the surface, were called 'people's palaces' in Soviet times, and their opulence is striking. Intricate designs, mosaics, statues: they ape and mirror the grandeur above ground. Exploring these hidden places, I began to see the city expanding and revealing itself, like a set of Russian dolls, one within the other.

So much of this place has been hidden. Though it was conceived as a perfect city, it seems today like a kind of Oz, where curtain covers curtain and mask hides mask. This St Petersburg once was Leningrad, once was Petrograd, once more was Petersburg. But that most recent name change was not so much a return or unveiling as the latest in a long series of cover-ups.

Over the centuries, it is not just the city that has changed its name, but streets and squares and buildings and bridges. Time and again they have been retitled and reinvented. Petersburg has been viewed by the country's leaders as an unfixed thing, a place that can be shaped and altered to the needs of the day. The most aggressive of these leaders, of course, were the Soviets, who tried to alter not just names but history too. They tore down churches or put them to new use. With sledgehammer irony, St Isaac's Cathedral was converted into a museum of atheism, while the Old

Believers Church of St Nicholas was turned into a museum of Arctic and Antarctic exploration. Inside, paintings and photographs of frozen landscapes now adorn the walls and ceiling. Religious icons have been replaced by dioramas and the clergy swapped for stuffed penguins and polar bears.

The communists built statues, then took them down again. They created monuments to selective memory, and to the terrible absence of doubt. And yet today, Stalin, who did so much to mould the history of this place, has in turn been hidden. The many tributes to him that once stood around the city now are gone. His face, so perfectly familiar, is now hard to find. Yet he is still there, walking the streets unseen. Concealed beneath shirts, on the chests of many older men, are tattoos of that face, tattoos which once would have demonstrated loyalty or perhaps offered protection against the firing squad, and which now exist only in mirrors and in the eyes of wives and loved ones.

Within the people of this city are millions of lifetimes of memories, and within those memories are the secrets that might once have led to exile or death, and which now are kept only out of habit. Those secrets are the dreams and nightmares of the city, what it was, what it is now and what it might have been. Millions of Petersburgs, of Leningrads, of Petrograds: fragments of the place, each no greater or lesser than the other. And beneath it all is the swampy ground and the broad, brown river.

*

In the city centre, looking out over the Neva, is a statue that is more than a statue. Unveiled in 1782 and dedicated from Catherine the Great to Peter the Great, the figure known as the Bronze Horseman has come to symbolise the city itself, the fate of one entangled forever with the fate of the other. As grand and imposing as one would expect from a monument such as this, the statue shows Peter atop a rearing steed, towering over all onlookers. He wears a toga and a laurel wreath, and beneath the hooves of his horse is a snake, symbolising evil and the nation's enemies. Designed by the French sculptor Etienne Maurice Falconet, the statue took sixteen years to complete, and the single piece of rippled granite it stands upon, weighing more than 1,500 tonnes, was dragged much of the way here by thousands of soldiers, a few agonising metres a day.

The story of the cursed city, and the natural and human disasters that have repeatedly threatened to make that curse come true, have echoed through Petersburg's three centuries. And for much of that time, this figure has been part of that story. Most famously, in one of Russia's best-known poems, Alexander Pushkin cemented the connection between statue and city, and cemented too the ambiguous place that both Peter and Petersburg have occupied in the national imagination. 'The Bronze Horseman' was written in 1833 and is largely set in the great flood that took place nine years earlier. It opens with a standard, mythologised account of the city's beginnings, admiring how this 'lovely wonder of the North' rose 'From darkest woods and swampy earth'. The poem then turns to the eve of the flood itself, when the river 'stormed and seethed' and, 'like a savage beast, leapt at / The city'. Here we meet the central character, a poor clerk named Yevgeny, who seeks out his fiancée's house only to find it destroyed by the rising water. The girl and her family have disappeared. Distraught, he wanders the city for months, never again returning home. In part two, set a year or more after the flood, we find Yevgeny stood before Peter's statue, with 'a tightness in his chest' and a 'boiling in his blood'. Enraged, he shouts at the tsar and then runs away in terror, while behind him, 'One arm flung out on high, full speed, / Comes the Bronze Horseman in his flight'. Yevgeny is pursued through the night by the living statue.

This is a poem riddled with tensions, ironies and contradictions. On the one hand it glorifies Peter and his creation,
while on the other it paints him as a tyrant, trampling the
ordinary man. Yevgeny, we are told, is the 'hero' of the story,
but Yevgeny is mad, pathetic and, by the end of the poem, lies
dead. Is the real hero not Peter, the great emperor, who made
this city and saved the nation with his strength and guile?

For his contemporaries, Pushkin's choice of setting would
have made these tensions clearer still, since this square was
the location of the failed Decembrist uprising of 1825 (the
year in which the poem's dramatic conclusion is also set). On
that occasion, three thousand soldiers and officers assembled
in an effort to stop Nicholas I from taking the throne after
the death of his brother Tsar Alexander. These rebels sought
a more liberal, freer Russia, with improved conditions for
their ordinary countrymen. It was a cause with which the
poet sympathised, and his closest friends were among the
insurgents. Pushkin himself would have been there, as he
later told the tsar, had he not already been in exile at the
time. But the coup was a disaster. More than a thousand
of those who gathered in the square were shot by troops
loyal to Nicholas. Of those who survived, many were sent
to Siberia, and five of the ringleaders were hanged. Political
repression in the country worsened under the new tsar as a
direct result, and Yevgeny's shout of anger in 'The Bronze
Horseman' echoed, if not directly paralleled, the Decembrists' own ultimately futile protest. And so statue and city
were entwined, and in literature as in life Petersburg took on
a dual character: both Paradise and Hell, both doomed and
fated for glory. This duality, as Pushkin and others recognised, came straight from the character of its founder. They
were the embodiment of Peter's own contradictions: hero
and villain, wise ruler and merciless despot.

Peter the Great was a giant of a man, literally and metaphorically. At over six foot seven, with legendary strength

and stamina, he was physically imposing. He was intelligent and brave – fearless, even – and he laid the foundations not just for this city but for the modern Russian state. Through his wisdom, skill and acuity, Russia was turned from a backward country into a significant and influential European empire. But Peter was also a profoundly strange person, cruel and sadistic. He took pleasure in tormenting prisoners – among them his own son Aleksey, whom he personally tortured for the young man's alleged patricidal intentions. The tsar was highly skilled in many trades, including carpentry and shipbuilding, but his hobbies also included dentistry, and Peter would regularly remove teeth from courtiers for his own amusement, then store these tiny trophies for posterity. He was cultured, and a bringer of Enlightenment values – he built the world's first public museum and founded the Academy of Sciences, as well as Russia's first library and school for non-nobles – but he was also an old-fashioned autocrat, utterly convinced of his own infallibility.

Most famous among his idiosyncrasies however, was the tsar's passion for what he called 'monsters'. For as well as collecting books, historical objects and art, Peter also gathered 'natural curiosities', alive and dead. These included dwarves, a hermaphrodite, Siamese twins, a multitude of deformed human and animal foetuses, a two-headed lamb and many other gruesome artefacts, which he pickled and put on public display. As his fascination with this collection grew, Peter declared that, by law, his subjects were required to donate to him any such 'monsters' they encountered. Many of these specimens can still be seen in the Kunstkammer on Vasilevsky Island.

It is difficult to think of another, comparable figure to Peter in recent Western history. A man who achieved so much at so great a price; a man whose myth – great as it is – is more than matched by his reality; a man who founded one of the world's great cities, but who did so in the most unlikely of locations. But here he is, Peter, in what is now called Decembrists' Square, facing out towards the river. Rearing up, his horse stands upon that symbol of evil, the snake, trampling the creature beneath its hooves. And yet, in a quirk of the sculptor's ingenious design, which has ultimately become part of its ambiguity, the horse is also supported by it – held in place, literally, by the serpent's coils. The statue celebrates a glorious emperor, but also a horseman of the apocalypse.

In Russia the question of who is the hero of Pushkin's poem is perhaps more complicated than it is for Western readers, who would tend, particularly today, to side with the trampled underdog. For here, the conflict is not just a narrative one, it is the central tension of Russian politics. Individual versus state, freedom versus power: these conflicts were unresolved for the poet, and they remain unresolved now. After centuries of repressive feudalism and more than seven decades of communism, it seems surprising, to Western minds at least, that Russians would be so quick to return to an autocratic style of government, repeatedly re-electing a leader who is in many ways akin to the leaders they left behind in the early 1990s. But the popularity of Vladimir Putin is undeniable. Despite protests from some quarters, and despite some suspicious election results, there seems little doubt that Putin and his style of democratic authoritarianism is supported by the majority of the Russian people.

As we sat on plastic chairs outside the Kazan Cathedral one afternoon, nursing bitter espressos procured from a coffee van, Mikhail Volkov told me something that, at first, I found shocking. 'Sometimes dictatorship works,' he said. 'Sometimes you need that kind of order.' I looked at him, unsure if he truly meant it, or if he was just trying to provoke me. I didn't respond, but waited for him to go on. 'Russia is a huge country,' he explained, 'and dictatorship might be the best thing for now. Putin created order out of chaos.'

Mikhail is an English teacher and occasional tour guide, in his late thirties. He is tall and handsome, and wears a baseball cap over his close-cropped hair. Intelligent, well-travelled and socially liberal, he doesn't conform to any stereotype I might have held of a typical Putin supporter. Speaking slowly, in almost perfect English, he seems to enjoy my surprise, and pauses dramatically before saying anything I might consider controversial. 'In the '90s we had chaos,' Mikhail told me. 'Everyone was just out for themselves. The big oil companies were privatised by individuals who made a lot of money – they were the oligarchs, like Roman Abramovich. People were just trying to get a house and a car of their own by whatever means they could. Then Putin came in and he said, "I know what you've been doing and how you made your money, but now you're going to have to play by the rules. And they're my rules".'

The transition from communism to capitalism in Russia was certainly a chaotic period. Many people saw their standard of living fall dramatically during the 1990s, as inflation and unemployment spiralled, while others made enormous fortunes from assets that had previously belonged to the state. Corruption was rife, and the safety net of the old system was replaced by an overwhelming sense of alienation and vulnerability. People could no longer rely on the certainties they'd once known. For more than seventy years, the country had – in theory, at least – shared a common goal, and a common set of values. Each citizen was – again, in theory – equal in worth to all others. When the Soviet era came to an end, though, all that changed. For those who did not experience that change first hand, it's hard to imagine the sense of disorientation that must have been felt by so many. It's therefore hard to imagine the relief with which Putin's arrival in politics at the end of the '90s was met.

Here was a man who offered an antidote to that disorder and disorientation; who seemed to promise a return to common ends and common means; who claimed that strong state power was the only guarantee of freedom.

And yet still it surprised me, the extent to which Mikhail was, if not exactly enthusiastic about what was happening, at the very least willing to overlook its flaws. He praised Putin, his achievements and style of governance, and dismissed his critics as irrelevant. He bemoaned the lack of political engagement across the country, but did little more than shrug his shoulders at the abuses of power of which he was in no doubt the government was guilty. He was angry about the re-emergence of the church as a political force in Russia, but refused to condemn Putin for exploiting religion for political gain. For Mikhail, as for many other Russians, the preservation of order and stability trumps all other concerns.

To the outside observer, this country can feel like a chaotic and unruly place. But that sense is not exclusive to those looking from elsewhere. Russians too are deeply aware of it. Perhaps, as Mikhail suggested, the country's size is partly to blame. It feels too vast and too disparate to be managed. But what's notable, regardless of the reason, is the extent to which, despite the upheavals the country went through at the beginning and end of the twentieth century, the nature of politics and power in Russia has remained the same, concentrated to a very great extent in the hands of one person. This is a country in which democracy is viewed by many as too unstable a system, the constant flip-flopping of power inconsistent with the desire and demand for order. It is a country that seems, constantly, to be battling with itself.

Nowhere else is this conflict between order and chaos so apparent as here in St Petersburg (of which both Putin and his right hand man Dmitry Medvedev are natives). This city was, from its very beginning, an imposition of order upon the chaotic land, a manifestation of human will and imperial power. Peter the Great imposed straight lines upon the islands and swamps of the Neva delta. He imagined canals where streams had run, he drew streets through the mud. The magnificence of this city was a direct response to the difficulty of its location. It was an act of defiance, not just against Russia's neighbours but against the country's own terrain. St Petersburg was conceived as an ideal city, but for a long time it remained a battleground, where flood and fire threatened to destroy what humans had created. And frequently, as Pushkin's poem describes, it was people who were on the losing side. Today, that battle feels less like one of man against nature than of man's desire for order against the chaos he creates: the chaos of poverty and corruption, of squalor and discontent, versus the order of authoritarianism and political power, of clean streets and brightly painted buildings.

On a drizzly afternoon I visited a museum dedicated to the short life of Alexander Pushkin, housed in the last building in which the poet lived, close to Palace Square. There were paintings, letters and furniture, as well as glass-fronted displays that recreated and retold episodes from his childhood in Moscow to the duel he fought in St Petersburg in 1837, in which he was shot and fatally wounded, dying two days later. The museum was cold and dusty, and when a stray column of light pierced the windows, I could see the motes glitter like a shoal of tiny raindrops, suspended. The place was virtually empty, apart from its staff – an army of elderly women, dressed in greys, browns and beige. By each doorway in the many rooms was a stool, and on each stool sat one of these women. As I walked through the museum, I felt their eyes follow me, observing everything. I noticed too that in every room, as I replaced the laminated information sheets provided in English, one of these attendants would swoop in to check the paper and to straighten it. I sensed a tut of disapproval following me as I walked, and I began to feel that, by being there, by lifting those sheets and then returning them, I was creating havoc.

I took to straightening the pages myself on the display cases, leaving them just as I had found them. I took care to ensure that each page was perfectly aligned, so that no fault could be found. Lingering close to the doorways I noted that the staff were still unable to resist their impulses. As I moved on, an attendant would invariably appear, approach the paper, only to find it just as it ought to be. Silently she would return to her seat, looking even more dissatisfied. Watching this strange ritual, I realised that the care I was taking was not what they had been hoping for at all. Their desire was not for straightness, it was for straightening. They did not wish to find order, but to impose it. I left them to it, then, and headed back out into the rain.

*

I decided to take a train to the north. I wanted to cross the parallel, which lies towards the edge of the city, but also to escape the noise and commotion for a few hours. I chose as my destination the village of Repino, almost, but not quite, at random. A resort on the Gulf of Finland, about twenty miles from the centre of St Petersburg, it seemed, I suppose, as good as anywhere. It had a museum dedicated to the artist Ilya Repin, after whom the village is named, and it would also have a view over the sea, which seemed like a good antidote to my urban weariness.

I found my way to Finland Station, the place where Lenin had returned to Russia in 1917 after his years in European exile, and where his statue still stands, draped in garlands of pigeon shit. After a discussion with the ticket vendor that was longer and more arduous than either of us would have liked, I found myself a space in a busy carriage. Squeezed in together on yellow plastic benches, my fellow travellers were *babushkas* doing crossword puzzles and young families shouting at each other, most seemingly on their way to weekend cottages in the country.

As the train pulled out from the station, an odd procession of people began to enter the carriage, all with goods to sell. First there was a selection of ice creams, then magazines and puzzle books, fake amber bracelets, torches, waterproof overalls, Russian and pirate flags, and jumping plastic spiders. As each seller arrived, they would stand at one end of the carriage and shout a sales pitch, like an air steward doing a safety demonstration. Then they would walk down the aisle in search of customers, though few appeared to sell anything at all. Some were good at their job, managing to be both loud and charming, but others seemed nervous – too quiet, or jittery, even. Perhaps they were new at the job, or perhaps it was just the latest in a line of failed careers. The worst of these vendors seemed pathetic and humiliated, as though worn down by the effort of the task.

Rumbling north, the train passed a succession of bleak industrial estates, some of which looked long abandoned. Crumbling factories, warehouses and chimneys; acres of rust and decay. Three inspectors arrived in the carriage then, with the smart uniform and menace of soldiers. Everyone hurried at once to find their tickets.

I showed mine and then closed my eyes for a moment to rest. When I opened them again we were among pines and grey-skinned birches. Here and there amid the forest a few houses could be seen, and sometimes a gathering of *dachas*. Some of these looked ramshackle and close to collapse, many years since their last encounter with paint. But others were smart and well-tended, with roses blooming all about. These dachas have long been a part of Russian life. In the eighteenth century they were gifts bestowed by the tsar upon loyal allies, country houses and estates to which ordinary people could never aspire. But after the revolution, when properties were nationalised, the Soviet authorities began to distribute them to community organisations. Restrictions were imposed on the size of dachas and their gardens in order to maintain the appearance of equality, and by the 1990s, when they were privatised once again, a great many families had one, usually on the outskirts of the city in which they lived. These dachas were used not just as retreats, where people could escape from the city at weekends and during holidays, but equally importantly, their gardens allowed people to provide themselves with vegetables and fruit, commodities that were often hard to come by during the food shortages that afflicted the country.

From the station at Repino I crossed the tracks to where a car park and a large modern building – half restaurant, half supermarket – stood. I looked around, in search of a direction. I was intending, somewhat vaguely, to find Penaty, the former home and studio of Ilya Repin. This is where he lived from the late nineteenth century until his death in 1930. When the area was ceded to Russia in the 1940s (it had previously been part of the Duchy of Finland, in the Russian Empire) it was named after its former resident.

Repin had been the most important and influential of the Wanderers, a group of artists dedicated to portraying the social problems and realities of their country. His most famous painting, *Barge Haulers on the Volga*, hangs now in the Russian Museum in St Petersburg. It portrays a group of peasants dragging a boat up the river, ropes tied over their shoulders. The faces of the men tell the story: of oppression, suffering and deprivation. The image is both beautiful and horrifying at once, a vision of social injustice that is, also, an explicit demand for change.

Repino seemed like a small place, but I had no map and there were no obvious signs that might point me in the right direction. Having walked back and forth around the building for a few moments, I returned to the car park, where elderly women were selling fruit and vegetables from pots and buckets on the street. In one corner of the car park was a noticeboard, and I scoured it for something helpful. Among a plethora of signs, I found one that was in English. It said, simply, 'This Way', with an arrow that pointed towards a lane in the forest. Other than these two words there was nothing I could understand. Nor was there anything to indicate what might be found in that direction. But since I had plenty of time and nowhere in particular to go, I followed it, enjoying the absence of logic in my choice. 'This Way' could lead anywhere at all, but anywhere was better than nowhere, and so I continued. I followed the path down the hill between the trees, noting the myriad little trails that branched off into the forest, to places unseen and unknown. A light rain shivered among the pines and dribbled down my neck and shoulders.

When I reached the end of the path another road lay in front of me. Beyond, I could see the sun glittering on the Gulf of Finland. I turned right and walked along the shore path. A wide golden beach stretches along this part of the coast, and offers somewhere to stroll for the spa visitors and rich dacha or apartment owners. Above the beach, expensive restaurants and hotels mingled with brand new apartments, some unfinished and advertising for owners. There was plenty of money in this town, it seemed. From the beach I looked out over the water, then turned to see the outline of the city to the south east, with the glittering dome of St Isaac's Cathedral clearly visible at its centre.

When the spas and restaurants thinned out I stopped and turned round, then tried the other direction. My feet and legs were getting wet and coated with sand from the path, and I was beginning to feel disheartened. Once or twice I walked down from the road to the beach to see if I could locate the museum from the sea side, but I couldn't, and so I just continued walking. Again, when the buildings thinned out I returned to where I'd first emerged from the forest. Without much thought I took another road that led away from the water, but again, in the end, I turned back without success. Twice I stopped to ask fellow walkers where I might find the museum, but each time I was met with a shake of the head and a 'Nyet!' It was impossible to know whether they'd failed to understand or whether they didn't know the answer. Or whether, even, they just didn't want to tell me.

By then I'd been walking for more than two hours and I still had no idea where I was going. I was searching for a building that I'd never seen before, in a place I didn't know, without a map, without directions, without a single clue. I realised then that I wasn't going to get there. I wasn't going to find what I was looking for.

Deflated, I walked back through the trees to the place where I had begun, at the restaurant and supermarket. My feet were damp and muddy and sandy. I felt hungry and irritated. I looked again at the noticeboard and its little arrow saying 'This way', and I made a mental note: the only sign you are able to read is not necessarily the right one.

Crossing the road back to the station, I stood on the platform waiting for the next train. Beside me, an elderly couple talked quietly to each other. In his hands, the man held a wicker basket, brimming with fat, golden mushrooms, plucked from the forest. Together we made our way back towards the city.

*

On a Sunday afternoon, in dappled sunshine, I stopped for a coffee on Yelagin Island, to the north of the city centre. The island is a popular weekend destination, a wooded park, with young people rollerblading and families out walking. Half-tame squirrels roamed the pathways, pursued by screeching children. The deciduous trees were turning

153

bronze and yellow, smouldering among the evergreens, and a chilly wind brought leaves and acorns tumbling to the ground.

I sat in the café courtyard looking out at a large metal cage, just across the path. The cage held three ravens, for the amusement of customers, most of whom ignored them. The birds stood apart from one another, each staring out in a different direction. They watched as people passed by, and sometimes they cawed pathetically out towards the trees. But there was nothing that could respond. There were no other ravens around. Everywhere I had travelled on the sixtieth parallel I had seen ravens. They are the great circumpolar bird, the avian natives of the north. At times they had felt rather like companions on this journey, and until that moment I had always found pleasure in the sight of them. Playful and intelligent, graceful and violent, they are creatures of both dreams and nightmares; they are scavengers and acrobats, murderers and artists, tricksters and prophets. I could not help but feel depressed by the sight of those three individuals, calling out to their imagined kindred. For them, home would always be in clear sight, but forever unreachable.

Like many people, I find myself both attracted and repelled by cities. I am drawn in by the choices they offer and by the freedom they promise, but I am left sometimes feeling lonely, particularly on short visits such as this one. In cities I can be struck, without warning, by a sense of alienation and by a feeling that, while there, I am separated from something important, or essential, even. When I finished university I moved, almost by accident, to Prague. I went for a month to train as a teacher of English as a foreign language, but at the end of my course I was offered a job and decided to stay. And so with little more than a shrug of my shoulders I found myself a resident of one of the most beautiful cities in Europe. It is a city that, over the year that followed, I came to know and to think of with intense fondness.

That year was one of the happiest of my life, but it was also one of the most surprising. Surprising because, in the midst of that happiness, caught up in the novelty of being where I was, something began to niggle at me. It was at first only a minor distraction, an encroachment on my least occupied moments, when my thoughts would turn north without warning. But it grew. Steadily, certainly, those thoughts grew. Until, in the end, I was almost obsessed. And this was not some vague, undirected nostalgia. This was not the ache I had known since I was ten years old. This was homesickness. It was a longing for one specific place: Shetland.

Though I had called the islands home for a long time by then, I don't think I had ever really imagined them as such. For years Shetland was just the place in which my family lived, and in which I stayed not really by choice but by necessity. It was not until I was in Prague that I really began to think about home, about what that word meant and why. 'Where are you from?' people would ask. 'I am from Shetland,' I said. But what did I mean by that? What did that 'from' imply, beyond the bare fact of my former residence in an archipelago of that name?

In Prague it occurred to me, I think for the first time, that it really did mean something. Previously my nostalgia had always been for things I couldn't bring back: for a childhood that was gone, in a place that would never be home again, with a father who was dead. But suddenly I understood that there was more to it: a bond I had not recognised before, or had refused to see. It was a thread or a leash, even, with me at one end and the islands at the other. Mad as it may seem, the thought that my homesickness could be pinned to a real place – to the place, indeed, that had been home for most of my life – was revelatory. I felt much as those ravens might feel if, after years of calling out hopelessly into the forest, they found that their cage door had been open all along. And so, after my year in Prague was up, I went home. And that, I suppose, was all I had ever wanted to do.

FINLAND and ÅLAND
neither one thing nor the other

Through a narrow crack in the curtains, I could see the morning coming to life. It was after eight but the sky was still dim, and paled by a haze of snow. From outside I could hear the squeal of metal on tarmac as ploughs roamed the streets, carving smooth trails through the night's fall. I drew the covers close around me and lay there in bed, listening, until I felt ready for the day.

I rose and showered, then reached into my bag for clothes. I pulled on two T-shirts, two pairs of socks, a pair of thermal long-johns, jeans and a thick, woollen jumper, then my jacket, scarf, hat and gloves. It was a ritual I undertook with anticipatory pleasure, because I like the cold. Not the blustery, biting chill of Shetland, but the calm, still degrees just below zero; the cold that fully fills the air, and necessitates the wearing of 'sensible clothes'. There is a cleanness to it, and a satisfaction that comes with the knowledge that it can be held at bay. The slap of frozen air against the face; the sharp gasp, deep in the lungs; the sting of pleasure that puckers the skin. It is as sensual and reviving as the thickest of tropical heats, and though I felt well-padded and well-prepared, I was looking forward to that first gulp of frost.

The town of Ekenäs lies at the very tip of Finland, south-west of Helsinki, where the body of the country peters out in a splutter of islets and skerries. In summer it is a tourist resort, offering access to the national park that sprawls across 5,000 hectares of the region's archipelago. Campers, kayakers, walkers and anglers can all find their fun around

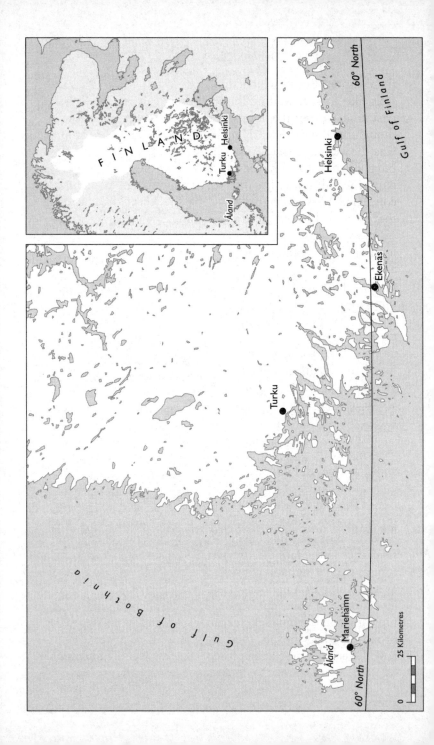

these shores. But in winter things are different. In winter it feels like a town waiting for something to happen. At half past nine, as I left the hotel, the light was still tentative, and though the flurries of early morning had ceased, an iron sky was glowering above. After the frantic rush of St Petersburg, Ekenäs was a haven of quiet. The snow muffled and dampened all noise. It gathered and enclosed, covered and concealed. It swaddled the town like the scarves and jackets that swaddled its red-faced pedestrians. Such weather insists on movement, on the necessity of keeping warm by activity, but thick clothing and icy pavements insist otherwise, and make moving difficult. So with heads bowed, the town's walkers hurried, slowly, in their various directions, breath billowing in the morning air.

As I trudged through the town, there were white piles of clean snow on the verges and brown piles of dirty snow along the kerbs. Winter turns orderly Nordic streets into messy thoroughfares. The pavements were slippery and uneven. Trees, in parks and in gardens, looked ghostly in their white coats. Conifers slouched beneath the frozen burden of their branches.

From somewhere nearby I could hear the ploughs still working their way through the town, mounding up the snow, as they did day after day. It is a Sisyphean task, this constant clearing of the streets. The snow falls and is shifted out of the way. More falls and that is shifted, too. Time and money are swallowed just pushing snow around, from one place to another. The Finns talk of *sisu*, a kind of stoic perseverance in the face of adversity. It is a stubbornness and a refusal to give in that is considered a personal quality as well as something of a national trait. And perhaps this might be an example of sisu right here: the men in their ploughs each morning and the families clearing drives and pathways with broad-mouthed shovels, then doing it all over again tomorrow. Over and over again tomorrow. Despite its practical necessity, this heroic repetition still feels faintly absurd and overwhelming. But perhaps, as Albert Camus concluded, 'One must imagine Sisyphus happy'.

Although there has most likely been a settlement in this area since at least the thirteenth century, the town of Ekenäs was officially born in the winter of 1546, by royal decree. At that time, as for much of its history, Finland was under the control of its neighbour to the west, and when the Swedish king, Gustav Vasa, decided to create a new town to compete for trade with Tallinn (then called Reval), Ekenäs was chosen to be that town. Money, materials and men were sent to the region to make the development as swift and effective as possible. And so it grew. But Gustav was not a patient man, and when Ekenäs failed after five years to live up to his expectations, he founded Helsinki a little further north, and concentrated his efforts there instead. Many of this town's early residents were ordered to relocate to the new settlement, and were not allowed to return until after Gustav's death.

For centuries, fishing was the main industry here, alongside the export of cattle, timber and animal hides. Craftsmen too began to congregate in the area – tailors, weavers, tanners, cobblers – and in the higgledy-piggledy lanes of the old town, streets still carry the names of the professions they once housed. There is Hattmakaregatan (hat-makers' street), Smedsgatan (smiths' street), Linvävaregatan (linen-weavers' street), Handskmakaregatan (glove-makers' street). The buildings too are named after the fish and animals that once would have driven the local economy: the eel house, the goat house, the bream, the roach and the herring.

Some mornings, Ekenäs felt stripped out, almost absent from itself, as though in winter the town didn't fully exist at all. I enjoyed exploring at those times, walking back and forth through the hushed streets, past the same shop windows and the same houses. Sometimes I walked out to the edge of town, where the trees took over, then turned back. I crossed the bridge to the little island of Kråkholmen, then turned again and headed to the Town Hall Square, where the sweet tang of antifreeze rose like cheap perfume from the parked cars.

At night things were quieter still. Parents and grand-parents dragged young children on sleds through the town centre, the snow lit like lemon ice beneath the streetlamps' glow. A few walkers, dog walkers, youths, couples and me: it was peaceful, and pleasant to be out. Only later on was the stillness broken, when boy racers practised handbrake turns at the icy junction outside my hotel, their cars spinning and sliding from one side of the road to the other.

Quietest of all, though, were the narrow streets and lanes of the old town, where footsteps creaked like leather on the trampled snow. Along Linvävaregatan, the oldest section, many of the houses were painted that earthy, Swedish red, with white window panels and features, while on nearby streets the boards were pastel blue, peach, olive and butter-scotch. In the garden of one of these houses, a male bullfinch, bright ochre-breasted, seemed almost aware of how perfectly he fitted in this colourful corner. The brightness of the town was completed by strings of Christmas lights slung over windows and trees. Though it was already mid-January, Yule wreaths were displayed on front doors, and electric candle bridges were arched behind glass. In Britain we rush to remove our seasonal decorations, to maintain an arbitrary tradition. Here, though, lights and candles are kept in place. They feel like a natural response to the cold and darkness, not just for Christmas but for the whole winter.

In a narrow lane in the old town, I stood one evening outside the small, square windows of a house. On the verti-cal weatherboards, the red paint was flaking away, leaving scars of age on the warped wood. Inside, there was no light, but I thought that I could make out two pictures hanging on the far wall: one a painting of a sailing ship, the other of a snowbound landscape. I could see only a few details of the room, but not the room itself. It looked abandoned, as though no one had been in there for years. It was an empty house that held a piece of the past intact. I am not sure what prompted me to want to take a photograph of this window. Perhaps it was the incompleteness of it, and the suggestion that, somehow, what lay beyond the glass was not entirely of the present. I wondered, maybe, if the lens might capture what I could not see, if it might illuminate the fragments and make them whole. But as I lifted the camera from my bag there was a movement inside, a shadow that crossed the space between me and those paintings. It looked like a person shuffling past in the darkness. I jumped back, as though I'd been caught doing something terrible, then turned and walked on, feeling guilty and unsettled. As the moments passed I found myself uncertain about what exactly I'd seen. Had there been a person there or had I only imagined it? I still can't say for certain.

*

Until the twentieth century, Finland had never existed as a nation, only as a culturally distinct region under the control of one or other of its powerful neighbours. Sweden occupied the territory from the mid-twelfth century up until the beginning of the nineteenth, but after the Napoleonic wars it was ceded to Russia, and became a semi-autonomous 'grand duchy'. In the century that followed, a cultural and political nationalism began to grow in the population. Although the Finnish parliament opened its doors in 1905 (and was the first in Europe to offer universal suffrage), it was not until more than a decade later that the country truly became a country. In the wake of the Russian revolution, Finland declared independence in December 1917, and despite the violence it had suffered at Russian hands in the past, it did not, in the end, have to fight for that independence. Lenin, who had spent time in hiding here from the tsarist authorities back in St Petersburg, was a supporter of Finnish nationalism, and one of his earliest acts as leader was to let the grand duchy go. Had his own history been a little different, the history of this country might also have been so. Though a short, bloody civil war ensued, between those who wished to emulate the new Russian socialism and those in favour of a monarchy, the country ultimately settled on neither, becoming instead an independent democratic republic.

Finland is often described as a strange place, one of the most culturally alien of European states, and in a sense that fact is remarkable. For despite being dominated from outside until just a century ago, this country always maintained an identity that was very much its own. That identity, and that very real sense of difference, was founded first of all upon linguistics. Contrary to a common misrepresentation, Finland is not a Scandinavian country, and its language is entirely unrelated either to those of its Nordic neighbours or to Russian. In fact, Finnish is not an Indo-European language at all. It is Uralic, and related therefore to Estonian and, more distantly, to Hungarian and Sami. However, this cultural odd-one-outness is complicated by the fact that, in parts of Finland, Swedish still predominates, with around five per cent of the population using it as their first language. This southwest region is one of those parts. Ekenäs is a Swedish town, and its Finnish name – Tammisaari – is far less commonly used by its residents. In cafés here, both languages rise from the tables, and nearly every sign, label and menu is printed both in Finnish and Swedish. This biculturalism is different from that of Greenland. For though they once would have been, these are no longer the dual languages of coloniser and colonised. These are two cultures existing side by side, complementary rather than competing. And the difference between the two is not one of national allegiance, either. Swedish speakers in Ekenäs do not consider themselves to be Swedes living in Finland but, rather, Swedish-speaking Finns. To me this seems a refreshing contrast to the simplistic vision of a national identity that is ethnically and culturally defined. It is an acknowledgement that identity – even linguistic identity – is always complicated. But of course, not everyone agrees.

In the centre of town, a row of boards displayed campaign posters for each of the eight presidential candidates in the forthcoming elections. These candidates included a representative of the Swedish People's Party, which fights to protect the interests of Swedish speakers, and also a candidate from the True Finns, a nationalist group hostile both to immigrants and to the Swedish minority. Supporters of the True Finns resent the continuing use of Swedish as an official second language, and its compulsory teaching in schools. They thrive on a lingering bitterness over the country's historical mistreatment by its neighbour. On a Friday night during my stay, in an act of quiet political sabotage, one of the True Finns' posters was removed from its board, and the face of their leader, Timo Soini, was torn from the other, leaving a blank hole that drew laughs of approval from shoppers the following morning. Though replacement posters had been put up by Saturday evening, those did not make it through the night unscathed either. Once again Soini's face was removed from one, while on the other a neat Hitler moustache was added. In a place as clean and graffiti-free as this, such vandalism was notable. Ekenäs clearly was not natural territory for the party.

In most nations, urban, literate culture has traditionally been valued more highly than rural or peasant culture, and Finland was once no different. But here, up until the nineteenth century, the culture of the town was Swedish, while the culture of the countryside was not. Finns were largely excluded from urban, economic life, and theirs for the most part was an oral culture, a culture of the home, the fields and the forest. After the annexation by Russia in 1809, however, things began to change. For the first time there was a sense that this rural culture could become a national one, and since they were keen to minimise Swedish influence in the territory, the Russians did nothing to discourage this new nationalism. And so, gradually, it grew.

Key to the rise of a rural, national, Finnish culture was the publication in the middle of the nineteenth century of a work of epic poetry called *The Kalevala*. This huge book, consisting of almost 23,000 lines, was based on the oral verse of the Karelia region, and was collected, collated and expanded by Elias Lönnrot, a doctor, who began his schooling in Ekenäs in 1814. Lönnrot brought together creation myths and heroic tales in a work of folklore and of literature. It was a deliberate attempt to set down a national narrative, comparable to the Icelandic sagas and Homeric epics. And though *The Kalevala* is less famous internationally than those predecessors, there is no doubt that within his own country Lönnrot succeeded. The book had an extraordinary influence, politically and culturally, and continues to do so even now. A national day of celebration, Kalevala Day, is held each 28th of February.

The oral poetry of Finland persisted into the nineteenth century not *despite* the fact that it was a suppressed language but *because* of it. The verses Lönnrot gathered were a kind of treasure that had been kept safe from harm in homes and villages across the region. And likewise, the survival of Finnish as a language and as a culture was possible precisely because its rural heartland was separate from the urban heartland of Swedish. The result of this geographical divergence was that, as a national culture came to be imagined and created, it was the countryside that was at its core. It was the landscape of Finland – the forests, lakes and islands – that shaped the nation's art, its music and its literature.

Though his first language was Swedish, Jean Sibelius was a fervent Finnish nationalist, and throughout his career he produced work directly inspired by *The Kalevala*. But it was nature that provided the energy and imagery that moved him most of all. It was that 'coming to life', he wrote, 'whose essence shall pervade everything I compose'. While working on his Fifth Symphony – the last movement of which was the only music to be heard in Glenn Gould's *The Idea of North* – Sibelius wrote that its adagio would be that of 'earth, worms and heartache'. And seeing swans fly overhead one day he found the key to that symphony's finale: 'Their call the same woodwind type as that of cranes, but without tremolo,' he wrote. 'The swan-call closer to trumpet . . . A low refrain reminiscent of a small child crying. Nature's Mysticism and Life's Angst! . . . Legato in the trumpets!' Gould, hearing this music in his native Canada, recognised something distinctively northern about it, something that chimed with the themes he wished to explore. It was, he said, 'the ideal backdrop for the transcendental regularity of isolation'.

*

On the broad pier down at the north harbour, summer restaurants stood abandoned, their outside tables, chairs and umbrellas deformed beneath six inches of snow. On one side of the pier, behind a tall metal gate, was a jetty that housed two public saunas, one for men and one for women. To the right of the jetty were the saunas themselves, and to the left was a square of sea enclosed between three platforms. Half of this square was covered by ice, like the rest of the harbour (the Baltic's low salinity means that it freezes more easily than most seas). But a patch beside the boardwalk was kept clear by a strong pump bubbling from below. Those few metres of ice-free water were the swimming pool.

I have swum in the sea in Shetland on many occasions, though mostly when I was young and stupid. That was cold. It was always cold, even on the warmest day. The Gulf Stream may keep the North Atlantic milder than it might otherwise be, but knee-deep in the waves, goose-pimpled and shivering, you would be hard-pressed to notice. But the difference between that cold and the cold of Ekenäs harbour was probably several degrees. And though I'd come to experience the sauna for myself, the idea of plunging into that ice-edged water, either before or after the heat, did not fill me with excitement. It was an experience that could surely be pleasurable only in hindsight: as something I *had* done, not as something I was *about* to do. And certainly not something I was in the process of doing.

The swimming, I'd been told, was optional, which was a relief. But beyond that, I really didn't know what I was supposed to do. There must be rules and protocols for a sauna, I thought. There are always rules and protocols for such culturally significant activities. I had assumed there would be other people whose lead I could follow, to avoid any serious lapses in social etiquette. But the only other guest was just leaving the changing room as I arrived, and so I was on my own. I'd read somewhere that most saunas do not permit the wearing of trunks, and so I'd not brought any. In fact, trunks had been pretty low on my list of things to pack for Finland in January, so I had none to wear even if I'd wanted to. Public nakedness is not something I have engaged in often, but in this case I was willing to do as is done, and so I stripped, opened the door to the shower room, and then went in to the sauna.

The room itself was just two metres deep and about the same wide, with wood panelling all over, and three slatted steps rising up from the entranceway. There were two windows on one side, and a metal heater was in the corner beside the door. On the top step, where I gingerly sat down, was a pail with an inch or two of water and a wooden ladle inside. I scooped a spoonful out and flung it onto the hot rocks. The stove screamed in protest. The temperature rose quickly in response, and steam curdled the air. An unfamiliar smell, sweet and tangy, filled the room: the smell of hot wood oils.

I sat back against the wall and looked out of the windows at the ice-covered sea. I was sweating from every pore, and my breath felt laboured on account of the steam. It was relaxing, but not entirely. One could rest, but not sleep. Again I wished for guidance: how long was I supposed to stay in the sauna? Was there something else I ought to be doing, other than just sitting? Was now the moment I should be throwing myself into the sea? I could hear people next door, in the women's sauna – there was laughter, and even the occasional shriek – but I could hardly pop in to ask for their advice. So instead I compromised and took a cold shower. It seemed suitable and not too cowardly an option. Open-mouthed and shaking hard, I stood beneath the flow of water for a moment that felt like an hour, my whole body trying to resist the ache of it. Then I rushed back into the sauna again, sweat bristling on my wet skin.

This ritual of intense heat and intense cold is considered a bringer of health, good for both mind and body. It has been part of the culture of this region for over a thousand years, and its importance is perhaps reflected in the fact that *sauna* is the only Finnish word to have found its way into common English usage. Today most Finns have one in their home, and many enjoy them at their workplace too. People socialise here; they have business meetings; and sometimes they just come to sit alone.

A sauna is an ideal place in which to be *omissa oloissaan*, or undisturbed in one's thoughts. Quiet contemplation is something of a national pastime here, instilled from childhood. 'One has to discover everything for oneself,' says Too-ticky, in Tove Jansson's *Moominland Midwinter*, 'and get over it all alone.' Silence and introspection are not just socially acceptable in Finland, they are considered positive and healthy. They are traits often misinterpreted by those from more talkative cultures as shyness or even bad manners.

Saunas mimic the Nordic climate – the heat of summer contrasted with the cold of winter – and when enjoyed at this time of year they hint at a kind of defiance or protest. To step into a little wooden room at eighty degrees celsius is to declare that even now, in darkest winter, we can be not just warm but roasting hot. We can make the sweat drip from our brows, then leap like maniacs into icy water. It is both an embrace of the season and a fist shaken in its face. It is a celebration of the north and an escape from its realities. The actress and writer Lady Constance Malleson went further. For her the sauna was 'an apotheosis of all experience: Purgatory and paradise; earth and fire; fire and water; sin and forgiveness.' It is also a great leveller, and appeals therefore to the spirit of Nordic egalitarianism. 'All men are created equal,' goes an old saying. 'But nowhere more so than in the sauna.'

After repeating this dash from cold shower to hot room twice more, I decided that I'd had enough. It was strangely exhausting, and I felt the need, then, to lie down. As I stood drying and dressing in the changing room, two men came in. They were in their sixties – one perhaps a little older. Both stripped down to trunks quickly, opened the door without a hesitation and went outside. I heard them splash into the sea, and a moment later they returned, dripping but not shivering, took their trunks off and went past me into the steam and heat next door. For a moment I considered turning round and joining them, as though I could shed my awkwardness by sharing others' ease. But I decided not to intrude on the silence of friends, and so I headed back out into the cold.

✳

From the centre of town I trudged ankle-deep down the tree-lined streets until, at the end of Östra Strandgatan, the trees took over. A woman and her little dog went ahead of me into the forest and I followed, treading carefully down the path. When she stopped to allow a procession of school-children to pet the dog I overtook and continued beneath the branches, their giggles and chatter rippling into silence behind me. This was the first of the town's nature parks – Hagen – with the islands of Ramsholmen and Högholmen, accessible by footbridge, lying beyond. The forest was mostly deciduous, so bare of leaves, but a map in my pocket identified some of the species: oak, wych elm, common hazel, horse chestnut, small-leaved lime, black alder, common ash, rowan, bird cherry. Away from the old town, with its colourful buildings, this place seemed altogether mono-chrome. Dark trunks against the white ground, beneath a bruised, grey sky. Even the birds – magpies, hooded crows and a flock of noisy jackdaws – added no colour.

I walked along the trail, through Hagen, then Ramsholmen, without purpose or hurry. The path was well maintained and trodden, though I could neither see nor hear anyone else around me. As I moved further from the town, the only sounds remaining were the patter and thud of snow clumps falling from branches to the ground, and the occasional bluster of birds somewhere above. Despite the absence of leaves, the canopy was dense enough to make it hard to see much at all, just now and then a flash of frozen sea emerging to my right. When I crossed the second foot-bridge, to Högholmen, the path faded, but still the snow was compacted by the footprints of previous walkers, and I continued to the island's end, where I could look out across the grey ice to the archipelago beyond.

In Finland, familiarity with nature is not just approved of, it is positively encouraged, and the state itself takes an active role in this encouragement. The path on which I had walked was well tended, despite the season, and street-lights had continued for much of the way, so even darkness couldn't interfere with a stroll in the forest. There were bird boxes everywhere, and benches, too, where one could stop and think and rest. The right to roam is enshrined in law in this country, as it is in the other Nordic nations. It is called, here, 'Everyman's right', and gives permission for any person to walk, ski, cycle, swim or camp on private land, no matter who owns it. Food such as berries and mushrooms can be gathered on that land, and boating and fishing are also allowed. The restriction of these rights by landowners is strictly prohibited. Indeed, the legal emphasis is not on the public to respect the sanctity of ownership, but on those with land to respect other people's right to use it. This means that, while land can still be bought and sold, it is a limited and non-exclusive kind of possession. The public, always, maintains a sense of ownership and of connection to places around them.

The emphasis on access and on the importance of the countryside in Finnish culture harks back to the rural nationalism of the nineteenth century. But it has become, in the twentieth and twenty-first centuries, a deep attachment to nature that finds its most notable expression in the profusion of summer-houses dotted around this country. Around a quarter of Finnish families own a second home or a cottage outside the town, and most have regular access to one. Often these are located on an island or beside a lake, and while many have no electricity or running water, nearly all are equipped with a sauna. This region alone has about five thousand of these cottages.

There is an old stereotype that says Finnish people, given the choice, will live as far apart from one another as possible, and perhaps there is a grain of truth in that. Perhaps the desire to remain close to nature necessitates a certain geographical distance from one's neighbours. But there seems to me something extraordinarily healthy in the attachment to place that is so prevalent here. There seems, moreover, something quite remarkable in this longing not for what is elsewhere but for what is nearby. It is an uncommon kind of placefulness that is surely the opposite of isolation.

On my way back towards town I stopped on the bridge between Högholmen and Ramsholmen. I took ham and rolls out of my bag and put together some crude sandwiches. I stamped my feet on the wooden planks to try and compensate for my gloveless state. As I stood eating, an old man in a bright green coat appeared from behind me. He must have been close by during my walk around Högholmen, though I never saw nor heard him once.

The man stopped beside me and gazed out over the frozen water. His face was soft and wrinkled, and a little sad, topped by grey, sagging eyebrows. His dark-rimmed spectacles seemed to hang precariously at the end of his nose, and yet, at the same time, they pinched his nostrils so tightly that his breathing must have been restricted.

'I've been looking for an eagle,' he said.

'A sea eagle?' I asked.

'Yes, a big one.' He extended his arms and flapped slowly, in demonstration of what a big sea eagle might look like in flight.

'I didn't see it today,' he explained, solemnly. 'But some days it is here.'

We stood together in silence for a moment, both looking in the same direction.

'Well,' he said, glancing up at the sky, 'it is fine now. But for how long?'

I smiled and nodded, recognising both subject and sentiment.

'What is coming tomorrow?' he added, turning away to go, then paused a second longer and shook his head, sadly. 'I don't know.'

*

Returning to Shetland from Prague in my mid-twenties was not the joyous homecoming I might quietly have hoped that it would be. It was difficult and tentative, and for a short time I questioned whether my decision had been sound at all. By then, my mother had moved away from Lerwick and away from the house in which I'd spent my teenage years, the house overlooking the harbour. Much had changed since then, and much was new to me. I had returned to Shetland because, finally, it had come to feel like home, but in those first few months a great deal again was unfamiliar.

Not long after coming back I got a job as a reporter for *The Shetland Times*, and a little flat in Lerwick, a few lanes away from where I'd been brought up. I settled in to a life that I felt I had chosen, and, as I walked through the town again, those buildings and those streets, those lines and those spaces, seemed as though they were etched inside of me.

In the months that followed I began to write every day, more than I had ever written before. I started work on what I thought was a novel: the story of a man's return to the islands after many years away. In that story, the man – I never chose a name for the character, he was simply 'the man' – reconnected himself with his home by walking, obsessively, the places he once knew. The steps he took not only rejoined him to the place, physically, they also drew him back, through his own history and into the history of the islands themselves. Or perhaps it would be more accurate to say that, through his physical connection, he drew the past upwards into the present. To fuel this work, I read books about Shetland history. I read novels and poetry. I visited the archives and the museum, and I learned much that I had never before been interested in learning. Through that anonymous character, I strove to relate myself to a place from which, previously, I had always maintained a distance.

It was then, in that time of research and writing, that I realised something which now seems obvious: that this history in which I was immersing myself was not separate from me. These islands' history could be my own. Though I had no connection by blood to Shetland, though my ancestors so far as I know had nothing whatsoever to do with the place, none of that truly mattered. The ancestors of whom I am aware lived in Norfolk and Cornwall and Ireland, places I know hardly at all. My connection to those places, carried in fragments of DNA, has little real meaning. Certainly it means nothing when compared to the connections I have made in my own lifetime. For culture and history are not carried in the blood. Nor is identity. These things are not inherited, they exist only through acquaintance and familiarity. They exist in attachment.

As I came to understand that fact, a sense of relief washed over me like a slow sigh, and I began to imagine that a matter had been settled and that something broken was on its way towards repair. By day, as a reporter, I wrote about Shetland's present; by night I read and wrote about its past. As familiarity and acquaintance grew, attachment brimmed within me.

*

In Turku, the country's second city, I boarded one of the enormous ferries that ply back and forth between Finland, Sweden and the Åland Islands. In the terminal, crowds had gathered in advance of departure time, laughing, talking cheerfully to each other, and once on board they filed into cafés, restaurants and – most popular of all – the duty-free shop. Soon, the ship was full of people, most of them weighed down by bags of alcohol and cigarettes.

Åland is separated from mainland Finland by a stretch of the Baltic that never fully unleashes itself from the land. From Turku we passed densely forested islands with bright summer houses at the shore. And though, as the morning progressed, the islands thinned out and decreased in size until an almost open sea stretched out around us, here still were holms and islets, some as smooth and subtle as whales' backs, just breaking the surface. From the boat, these islands looked as though they had just risen up from beneath the water – which in fact many have. The land here is rising at fifty centimetres per century, so new islands are emerging all the time. And when they do so, it doesn't take long before they are occupied by trees. Even the smallest of skerries, it seemed, had at least one rising from it. Coming from a place where such extravagant vegetation needs to be coaxed and coddled from the ground, it was amazing to see this profusion. In the Baltic, trees won't take no for an answer.

The sixtieth parallel runs through the south of the Åland archipelago, not far from the capital, Mariehamn, where we docked around lunchtime. Disembarking, with rucksack slung over my shoulder, I was surprised to see most of my fellow passengers walk out from the ferry and then straight back on to another one heading in the opposite direction. For the majority, it turns out, the journey is simply the first half of a full day's cruise to Åland and back, with good food and tax-free shopping more important than the destination. I stepped out into the town's grey winter light and headed for my hotel.

If there is ambiguity in the relationship between Swedish Finns and the state in which they live, in Åland the situation is rather different. Here, there is less ambiguity and more complexity. These islands belong, officially, to Finland, but they are culturally Swedish and politically autonomous. The residents are highly independent-minded. The archipelago has its own parliament, its own bank, its own flag and its own unique system of government. Despite a population of fewer than 30,000, spread over 65 inhabited islands, Åland has the power to legislate on areas such as education, health

care, the environment, policing, transport and communica-
tions. It is, to all extents and purposes, a tiny state operating
within a larger one, and its separation from that larger state is
fiercely maintained. Finnish is not an official language in these
islands, and the army of Finland is not welcome on its shores.

This strange situation did not come about because of a
long-held sense of nationhood here (unlike, say, in the Faroe
Islands). Instead, it was the result of a peculiar and, in hindsight, rather enlightened decision by the League of Nations.
For centuries these islands had been a de facto part of Sweden,
but in 1809 they were annexed together with Finland. Åland
became, then, part of the grand duchy that survived until
the revolution of 1917. At that time, as Finland prepared to
announce its own independence, Ålanders demanded that
the islands should be returned to Sweden, both for reasons
of cultural continuity and to be brought under the protection of an established and stable state. But given the history
of this region, the request was not a simple one to grant,
and when the three sides failed to agree, the matter was
referred instead to the League of Nations. In attempting to
come up with a solution that would please everyone, the
League settled on a compromise. Rather than staying with
one state or joining another, Åland would instead become
autonomous and demilitarised. It would function within the
state of Finland, but its Swedishness would be enshrined
in law. It would be, in other words, neither one thing nor
the other. Such a precarious compromise could easily have
been a disaster, but in this case it was not. In fact, it turned
out remarkably well. Today islanders are proud of their
autonomy and what they have done with it. They maintain
strong links with both neighbours, but have fostered and
cultivated a sense of distinctiveness and independence that
is now, almost a century later, firmly embedded.

Mariehamn sits on a long peninsula, with a deep harbour
on one side where the ferries come in and a shallow one on

the other, for pleasure craft. In the smaller harbour, expensive boats were hidden beneath plastic wrappers, while the wharf was chock-a-block with empty spaces, to be filled by summer visitors.

I strolled across the bridge to Lilla Holmen, a snowy, wooded park that was more or less empty of people. An aviary stood among the trees there, teeming with zebra finches, budgerigars, parrots and love birds, and there was even a tortoise, lying still in the corner. Outside in the park were giant rabbits in hutches, and three peacocks that approached me, then raised and shook their fans as though in protest.

There is an unmistakable air of self-confidence to Mariehamn. The town feels like what it almost is: the capital of a tiny Nordic nation. The wide linden-lined boulevards; the grand clapboard villas; the lively, pedestrianised streets: Mariehamn pulses with a kind of energy that belies its scale. Just 11,000 people live in this town, and yet it seems many times bigger. It feels creative and vibrant and prosperous. In the summer this place would be full of visitors – Finns and Scandinavians, mostly – but in January there were few of us around. Yet unlike in Ekenäs, that didn't feel like a loss. There was no sense of limbo, or of absence. Tourists bring money to the islands, but they don't bring purpose. Åland's focus is upon itself and its own concerns. After all, how many other communities of 28,000 can boast two daily newspapers, two commercial radio stations and one public service broadcaster?

I couldn't help comparing this place with home, and with Shetland's own capital, Lerwick. As I wandered Mariehamn's rather grand streets I thought of the streets in which I grew up. In the time I've known it, my home town has changed significantly, and despite the islands' wealth it has begun to look a little run down. An enormous supermarket on the edge of town has sucked much of the life from its centre. Once home to a host of independent businesses, the town's main shopping street is now a place of hairdressers and charity shops, and Lerwick's museum and its recently-built arts centre are outstanding in part because of what they are set against.

I wondered then, as I have often wondered, whether more autonomy could have brought some of the benefits to Shetland that Åland has seen, and I think perhaps it could. But Åland's success has been bolstered by two factors that are not on Shetland's side: geography and climate. These islands are not just beautiful, they are also sunny and warm in summer, and therefore very popular with tourists. Åland is also fortunate to lie halfway between two wealthy countries, and a tax agreement means that Finns and Swedes can take day cruises here and come home with bags full of cheap booze. Åland is politically autonomous, but it is still financially reliant on its neighbours. In the 1930s, the largest fleet of sailing ships in the world was owned by the Åland businessman Gustaf Erikson, and the economy is still very much dependent on the sea. The ferries which today carry around a million passengers each year back and forth across the Gulf of Bothnia are, by a considerable margin, these islands' biggest industry.

＊

Wandering on a half-faded afternoon, I stepped on impulse in to the Åland Emigrants Institute, which occupies an unassuming building set back from Norre Esplanadgaten, one of the main streets in the centre of town. I'd read somewhere that there was an exhibition inside, but the institute is not a promising looking place and it wasn't clear if visitors were actually welcome. Inside there was little to indicate whether I was in the right place at all, just a narrow hallway and corridor with an office at the far end, its door open. I turned to go again, disappointed, but was stopped as I did so by a woman beckoning me back. 'It's not really an exhibition,' she said, in answer to my question. 'It's just a few things. But do come in anyway.'

The office was cramped. Inside were two large desks facing each other, with books and files and folders stacked everywhere around the room. The exhibition, as warned, consisted of a few odds and ends – some old photographs, crockery and medals – but I wasn't really shown any of it. Instead I was sat down, offered a cup of tea, then bombarded with questions.

The woman who had shown me in was Eva Meyer, the director of the institute, and her colleague at the other desk was Maria Jarlsdotter Enckell, a researcher. Eva was middle-aged, quiet and attentive; Maria was in her seventies, with well-tended white hair, and a pair of glasses clutched in her hands. As I sipped at my tea, the two women asked about my travels. Where was I from? Where had I been? Where was I going next? Why was I doing it? We spoke about the sixtieth parallel, and about the countries through which it passed. They liked the idea of my journey, they told me; they liked the connections that it made. Eva took a globe from the corner of the room and returned to her desk, turning it slowly as we spoke, her finger following the line. Both women had been to Alaska recently, they said, to attend a conference about Russian America. I told them about my own time there, and about the village of Ninilchik, with its little Orthodox church. Eva and Maria looked at each other, their eyes widening. 'Ninilchik? Really?' they asked. I nodded and waited for an explanation.

I had arrived at the institute at 3.30 p.m., half an hour before it was supposed to close. But at four o'clock Maria and Eva were only just beginning their story. The place of Finns in Russian history, they told me, had been vastly underestimated, particularly in terms of its colonial expansion. After all, at the beginning of the nineteenth century, Russia was still struggling to man its overseas developments.

St Petersburg was only a hundred years old, and the country simply didn't have enough trained and experienced seamen. Residents of the grand duchy, with its longer maritime history, were extremely useful and often were willing recruits. The Russian American Company offered Finns the security of a seven-year contract in Alaska, with as much salmon as they could eat, as well as an annual salary and accommodation. By signing on as mariners, or with other trades and skills, the men would have a chance to climb in society, working their way up from cabin boy to skipper.

Maria told me the story of one such recruit, Jacob Johan Knagg, who was born at Fagervik, close to Ekenäs, in 1796. By the time he came of age, Finland was under Russian control, and with his mother dead and his father remarried, Knagg decided to go abroad. He left Finland first for Estonia, on a trading ship owned by the local ironworks, but at some stage – probably around the end of the 1820s – he must have joined the Russian American Company.

In 1842, Knagg was working on a cattle farm on Kodiak Island along with his wife, whom he probably met in Alaska. Six years later he applied for colonial citizenship – an application that was ultimately successful. By that time, he was reaching retirement age, and as was customary he was discharged with enough food to last for a year, plus the equipment and supplies he would need to build a home. The Knagg family were then sent to the newest Russian settlement in Alaska. Which is where, in the summer of 1851, Jacob Johan Knagg died, leaving behind his wife and seven children. That settlement was Ninilchik.

Every so often, Eva or Maria would search for something to help illustrate the story. They brought out files, lists of names and family trees. According to Maria, as many as a third of 'Russians' in Alaska were not Russian at all; they were Finns, Estonians, Latvians, Danes and Poles. There was a deliberate attempt, she said, to minimise and even deny this fact, because it didn't fit with Russia's official, patriotic story. Historians in North America too were reluctant to accept her research, Maria explained. They had, she told me, been 'blinded by politics'. Much of her work now was an attempt to prove what she already believed: that a significant number of Finnish migrants arrived in Alaska decades before the great waves of European migration swept westward across the Atlantic. Together with their descendants still living in the state, she was tracing the stories of men and women such as the Knaggs, and drawing new lines in the process, between here and there, between now and then.

At half-past six, when the talk had come to a natural pause, the pair insisted we should eat. 'We will be having . . . stuff,' Eva said. 'Picnic style.' She put her coat on and headed for the door. 'We have lots of things to eat, but I will just go out and get some dessert.'

Half an hour later, we sat down together at a little table in the hallway, strewn with food. We ate chicken legs, salad, fruit and bread rolls, and drank cranberry juice to wash it down. Then we returned to the office and to the conversation.

In that room, filled with fragments of the past, time seemed to tighten and turn back on itself. The space was crammed with stories of those who had left their homes, reluctantly or by choice, for a life elsewhere. It was crammed, too, with the stories of those, here and around the world, who were trying to learn something of their family's past. Eva and Maria took great pleasure in bringing those pasts back to people, telling them who their ancestors had been, where they had gone and how they had lived.

At half past nine, six hours after I had arrived, Eva and Maria sent me back out into the evening, wishing me well on my travels. In my hands I clutched the twin tokens of their generosity: a bag of files and papers in one, a bag of bananas in the other.

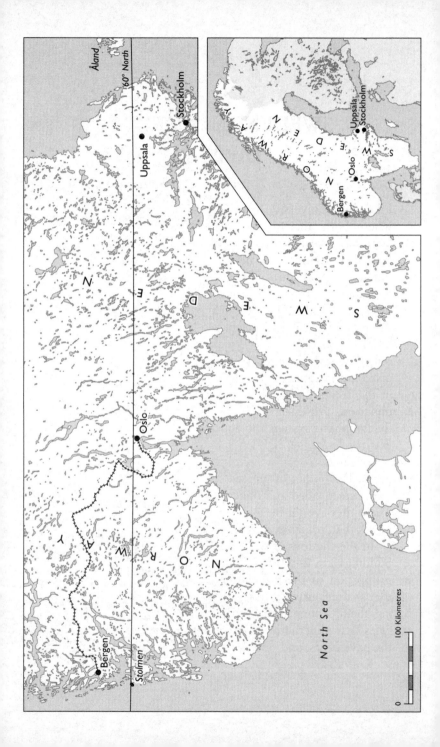

SWEDEN and NORWAY
last lands

Like many university towns, Uppsala has the feel of somewhere both ancient and youthful at once. A centre of
learning since the fifteenth century, and of religion for at
least a thousand years before that, this has long been the
intellectual and spiritual heart of Sweden. The city's skyline
is dominated by two historic landmarks: the Gothic, red-
brick cathedral – the tallest in all the Nordic countries – and
the rosy pink castle that sits on higher ground, just a few
hundred yards away. In the centre, a third building stands
out: the Gustavianum, whose unmistakable cupola of oxi-
dised green, topped by a globe, was built by Olof Rudbeck
in the 1660s. Inside that space, high above the streets, the
illustrious professor – who began his career by discovering
the lymphatic system and ended it by claiming that Swedish
was the language of Eden and Uppsala the site of Atlantis
– pioneered dissection techniques under the gaze of his students. The bodies of hanged criminals would be brought in
to the steep-sided anatomical theatre and laid upon a table.
There they would be taken apart, to better understand the
pieces that, together, make up a life.

In the shadow of these and the city's many other grand
buildings are 24,000 students, who make up a significant
proportion of the population. And on the cobbled streets
that shatter outward from the River Fyris, there is no escap-
ing them. Young, beautiful people gather in the bars and
cafés that punctuate the city; they shiver arm-in-arm along
the pavements, and pose for photographs in their black and

white 'Uppsala caps'. Everywhere, their bikes carve runnels through the slush, and sputter filthy arcs into the air behind. Like Oxford, like Prague, like Copenhagen, this is a very youthful old city.

On my first morning in Sweden, I stopped beside the river, where a narrow fish ladder – built for migratory asp – bypasses the weir. There, a dipper was perched upon one of the ladder boards, ducking and bobbing like a tiny boxer. Again and again the bird would bow its head under the flowing water, then submerge itself completely. Up it would come, with a flicker and fluster, then down again, its white throat and breast winking in the grey air. Around me, the snow was falling in fat lumps, all puffy and swollen, yet with crystals as clear as if they were caught beneath a magnifying glass. I stood watching the bird as the flakes settled on my shoulders, cheeks and eyelashes, until I could ignore the cold no longer.

Inside the cathedral, a few moments' walk away, I closed the door and a kind of stillness descended. The place was almost silent and almost empty. The only other person I could see was a hunched cleaner, mopping and polishing the flagstone floor. As she moved back and forth with her eyes to the ground, I stood looking the other way, the great pillars dragging my eyes upwards, towards a sky that was just beyond seeing.

Inside this cathedral are buried some of the city's most famous former inhabitants. In the Lady Chapel at the far end lies King Gustav Vasa. The walls of that chapel are adorned with murals depicting scenes from the king's life; the starstudded ceiling, a glorious eggshell blue, hangs like a pardon over the extravagant sarcophagus. Elsewhere in the cathedral are the relics of Saint Erik, an earlier king, as well as those of Bridget, the country's patron saint. The scientist and philosopher Emmanuel Swedenborg lies in the Salsta Chapel, and Olof Rudbeck is buried beside the central altar.

Close to the entranceway, a plain, unadorned stone marks the grave of Carl von Linne, or Linneaus, who died in 1778. Physician, botanist and biologist, he was the creator of modern taxonomy. Under his system, each species of animal and plant was part of a kingdom, class, order, family and genus. It was Linneaus who finally separated the whales from the fish, and it was Linneaus who brought human beings together with the apes. His system, like Rudbeck's dissections, both divided and connected the world.

*

In those first few months after my return from Prague to Shetland, as I worked and walked and wrote, reacquainting myself with the home that finally felt like home, I thought I had reached a point at which I could stop. For years I had felt like a moth, drawn in by lights that were no use to me, and held back by panes of glass I could neither see nor comprehend. I had blustered this way and that, confused and lost. But now I was back – back where I had been, years earlier, only this time by choice. This time the direction had been my own. In those first few months I didn't imagine that this return would be temporary, that within a year I would have moved again. In those first few months, I didn't account for love.

I fell in love with Fair Isle the moment I arrived there. Or perhaps it was earlier still, on the ferry, as we approached the island and it grew from an indistinct shape on the horizon into something both complete and completing, something that felt as though it was already a part of me, and had always been so. It was as intense and surprising a feeling as that which had struck me in Kamchatka – more so, in fact. Only this time the feeling was directed somewhere closer, more attainable.

That first trip to Fair Isle lasted only two days, but its impact on me was enormous, and in the year that I came back to Shetland I began to visit every fortnight. My brother was working at the bird observatory there that summer, which gave me both opportunity and excuse. And then I met a girl. She had grown up on the island, and through her I came to know it better. Each time I made that journey, by boat or by plane, I felt a kind of relief, as though I were going back to a place in which I felt more fully myself. And when the opportunity arose for that girl and I to move to the island, I didn't hesitate. There seemed nothing more natural and more logical to me at that moment than to go. And so Fair Isle, three miles long by one and a half miles wide, and separated from Shetland by twenty-five miles of water, became my home.

It is impossible to untangle attraction. We are drawn in our various directions for reasons both inexplicable and inexpressible. We desire what others find repellent; we cling on to what others do not want; we are magnets with unpredictable poles. What I found in Fair Isle was a place that was both new and familiar at once, both nearby and far away. Like Fort Smith, it was a place, too, that was utterly central to itself. Though it is in theory the most remote inhabited island in Britain, and though on many days of the year one can look out and see no other land at all, it never felt remote to me. In Fair Isle, it was other places that were far away. The island itself was exactly where it ought to be. That feeling of deep centredness and settledness suited me. Here was somewhere I did not feel torn or pulled in opposing directions. Here was somewhere I could just be.

Most of all, though, it was Fair Isle's community that drew me in. It was the connections that people had with each other and with their place – connections that were obvious to even the briefest of visitors. To live in Fair Isle was unlike living anywhere that I had known before. It was to become a member of something bigger and more important than any individual. It was to belong to a community that was greater than the sum of its parts, independent from and yet dependent upon each member. On that island, among those people, I came to understand and to experience a sense of attachment that was stronger, more intricate and yet somehow simpler than any I had felt before. Fair Isle was the first place in which my desire to be at home felt welcomed and reciprocated. It was the first place in which that desire that had dogged me for most of my life truly identified itself. An unanswerable longing took shape, then, and that shape became its own answer.

I moved to Fair Isle with no particular idea of how I might survive financially. With a population of less than seventy, there are just two or three full-time jobs on the island; everyone else has several part-time roles that, together, constitute a living. Every service that elsewhere is taken for granted, there must be carried out by the same few people. Every role must be filled, or the whole cannot work. I began my time on the island by joining the knitwear co-operative and learning how to operate a knitting machine. It was a process for which I had no particular aptitude. In my first winter, I made hats and scarves, a couple of jumpers and a cardigan, which were sold to visitors the following summer, and are probably still in use somewhere in the world. But I didn't stick to the knitting for long once other opportunities arose. I became a road worker next – digging ditches, filling potholes, pouring tar, shovelling grit in the winter – and I worked a few hours each week as a classroom assistant in the primary school. At the end of my first year, I began editing a magazine in Shetland, which I could do from home and fit in around my other roles. I kept a couple of dozen sheep among the communal herd on the hill; I joined the coastguard cliff rescue team; and towards the end of my three years on the island I worked as an occasional deckhand on the ferry, *Good Shepherd IV*. Almost every day I could wake up and do something different from the day before. It suited me better than I ever could have imagined.

When I lived in Fair Isle, I felt proud to be part of something that I believed in completely; and I still believe in it, though I am no longer there. That island came to mean more than any other place to me; that community left me changed forever. When I think of Fair Isle, as I do almost every day, each thought is bound by gratitude and by love, and each thought is sharpened by the memory of leaving. When I moved away, after three years on the island, it was with intense sadness. But I did so because, to put it simply, I was no longer fully there. For the last of those years I was living alone, and that was a long way from ideal. I began to miss my family and friends in Shetland, and I began to spend more time visiting them. Were Fair Isle more accessible, that would not have been a problem. But Fair Isle is not accessible. Travelling back and forth is difficult and expensive, and the weather makes it unreliable. The island can be cut off for days at any time of year, and in the winter it can be weeks. In the end I took what seemed like the most sensible option, and I moved back to Shetland. It was one of the hardest things I have ever had to do.

*

Beneath dim orange lights in a corner of the University of Uppsala's library building, the Carolina Rediviva, hangs a glass-fronted case, and inside that case is a map. At 1.7 metres wide and 1.25 metres tall, the map is impressive in its scale, but it's even more so in its content. Though slightly faded and honeyed by age, the image itself is clear. It shows the northernmost parts of Europe – the Nordic countries, the Baltic region, Scotland and Iceland – and it shows them all in their right places. Known as the *Carta Marina*, and printed in Italy in 1539, this was in fact the earliest map to show the north with such a degree of accuracy. A masterpiece of cartography, it was created by Olaus Magnus, a Swede living in exile in Rome.

Olaus Magnus was born in Linköping, southern Sweden, in 1490. He was educated in the church and became a Catholic priest, employed by Gustav Vasa for diplomatic work in Scandinavia and on the continent. When the Protestant Reformation began in Sweden in the late 1520s, however, Olaus and his brother Johannes, then archbishop of Uppsala, were forced to flee, and their possessions were confiscated. The pair finally settled together in Rome, and when Johannes died in 1544 Olaus was given the title – by then entirely symbolic – of archbishop. He was unable to ever visit this city or his home country again.

Despite this, Olaus remained obsessed with Sweden and the north. He produced the *Carta Marina* in the early years of his Italian exile, and then in 1555 he published his *History of the Northern Peoples*, a work in twenty-two books that brought together much of the information and misinformation about the region that was then in existence. It covered politics, geography, history, natural history and folklore, alongside observations based on his own extensive travels. It was for a long time the most significant and widely-read work available on the north, and together with this map comprised something like an extended love letter to his homeland. According to Barbara Sjoholm, both 'are products of an exile's recollection and imagination, produced in part to make a case for his country, and also as an act of memory and longing.'

The *Carta Marina* almost disappeared forever, after all of the known originals were lost before the end of the sixteenth century. But in 1886, one was located in Munich, where it remains today. And in 1961, another was found in Switzerland. That copy – this copy – was purchased immediately by the University of Uppsala and brought back to where, in a sense, it belonged.

The map is illustrated with an extraordinary degree of detail. Each country is adorned not just with place names and geographical features, but also with buildings, animals and people. Uppsala is there, with its cathedral clearly visible; so too is the castle at Raseborg in Finland, close to where Ekenäs would be built shortly after the map was produced. At the southern tip of Greenland, a Norseman and Inuit are fighting; and in the eastern Baltic, Swedish and Russian troops face each other across the water. But the map, like the books, blends together the familiar with the mythical. In the far north and in the ocean, geography and fantasy become entwined. More than a dozen marine monsters populate the North Atlantic – some of them attacking ships, some attacking each other. Several of these creatures are presumably whales, drawn by someone who had never seen a whale. Others have less obvious origins. According to the map's Latin key, these include 'Rosmarus, a sea elephant' and 'The terrible sea-monster Ziphius', which boasts a tall fin, stripes, a spiny mane and webbed feet. At its side is 'Another grisly monster, name unknown'. The ocean, according to the *Carta Marina*, is a terrifying place to be.

Somewhat to the left of the map's centre is my home. Unlike the outline of Scandinavia, Shetland is not drawn with much accuracy. It looks rather like a boiled egg, sliced into six pieces. 'The Hetlandic islands and bishopric [are] a fertile country,' the key declares, and they boast 'the most beautiful women'. But Olaus clearly did have access to reliable information about the islands because, of the few place names he includes, most are still recognisable. The island of Mui on the east coast is likely to be Mousa, and Brystsund is surely Bressay Sound, on the shores of which Lerwick would later be built. Skalvogh is Scalloway, which would have been capital of the islands at that time, and Svinborhovit in the far south is Sumburgh Head. The little island just below – Feedero – is Fair Isle.

What is striking about the *Carta Marina* is that it shows the north not as an empty, desolate region, as many in

Mediterranean Europe would still have imagined it, but as a place bursting with activity and life: animal life, marine life, human life. This is a map that seems to pulse rather than lie still; it is a restless, dynamic image, infused with the energy of the world it depicts. No one else was in the room with me that morning, and for a long time I stood gazing at it, exploring those shapes and spaces that were at once so familiar and yet so unlike the cartography of today. The purpose of this map was to do more than educate; it was to inspire a reimagining of place, and to turn southern heads towards the north. Despite its many distractions – the beautiful and the monstrous – my own head kept turning towards home.

*

On a bright, Sunday afternoon I walked from the cathedral down to the river bank, then northwards on the pilgrims' trail towards Gamla ('Old') Uppsala. This is the path along which the remains of King Erik Jedvardsson – later, St Erik – are supposed to have been carried in 1167, towards their final resting-place in the city. The trail follows the river Fyris, where mallards skulked among the frosted bulrushes, then it turns away into the fringes of the city, past a bowling alley, sports centre and car park. Neat rows of tiny cottages and allotments, all closed up for the winter, lead on through tree-lined lanes and smart housing schemes, their windows glittering in the icy sunlight. The trail was busy, despite the cold. Children in down jackets dragged plastic sledges behind them, while parents pushed prams in front; lovers strolled hand in hand, joggers panted past, and elderly couples took careful steps, their walking poles clacking like magpies against the pavement. All of us were headed in the same direction, away from the city, to where the day would open out. Across a busy road, then down a lane, past sleepy bungalows and gardens, the landscape began to change.

Trees replaced buildings, and a series of low hillocks rose up on one side of the path. Out ahead, flat white fields stretched towards the horizon.

I left the main trail there and walked up towards the edge of the trees, where several boulders stood, each with coloured pebbles glued on top. According to a leaflet I found nearby this was a 'place of meditation', and the pebbles were 'pearls of life'. They were, it said, 'an aid for modern pilgrims. For the greatest and most significant of all journeys – the journey inwards'. I thought about that label – 'modern pilgrim' – and wondered if it could apply to me. I hoped not, for the mawkishness of it made me wince. But still, the question lingered. There I was, treading a long road towards where, exactly? Looking for what? I'd often on these journeys felt uneasy about my motives and my desires. I'd often questioned what I was doing, and what I was trying to do. But I'd never once thought of myself as a pilgrim. So if that's what I was, I was either an accidental or a dishonest one, a pilgrim guarding himself against disappointment. For a few moments I stood there, unmoving, as a woodpecker thrummed nearby and a pair of nuthatches scraped at the corrugated bark of a pine.

Returning to the path below, I continued northward through thinning light. The sky was a broad, watery blue, broken only by vapour trails crisscrossing above. The sun slouched over the western horizon, with a pale yellow glow that dragged gangly shadows across the landscape. Everything was more clearly defined in this light; everything seemed more certain of itself. The fields were striped by ski trails and by the memory of ploughs. The stalks of last year's crop protruded through the snow like the stubborn bristle of a day-old shave. From there I could see what I had come to see: three gently-sloping lumps, with a stone church beyond. These were the 'Mounds of the Kings' or 'Royal Mounds', one of the most important archaeological sites in all of Scandinavia, and looking out towards them I was struck by two conflicting feelings. The first stemmed from the knowledge that this is an important place – a sacred place, even. Such knowledge brings with it a kind of wonder and mystery, and Gamla Uppsala certainly has both. Yet at the same time that feeling was contradicted by the utterly unexceptional appearance of the place, by the tameness and the tediousness of it. The 'Mounds of the Kings' are precisely that – mounds – and are neither dramatic nor particularly engaging, in and of themselves. Were it not for the flatness of the surrounding land, these tumuli would be barely noticeable at all. As it is, they stand out like ripples in a millpond.

It takes a fair leap of the imagination to conjure up, in this place, the scene described by Adam of Bremen in the late eleventh century. Furnished, he claims, with eyewitness accounts, Adam described a temple then standing on this site that was 'entirely decked out in gold'. Here, 'the people worship the statues of three gods', called Thor, Wotan (Odin) and Frikko (Freyr), the last of which was built 'with an immense phallus'. But as if a giant penis were not bad enough, Adam also reported that during midwinter feasts at this temple, human and animal sacrifices were made. '[Of] every living thing that is male,' he wrote, 'they offer nine heads, with the blood of which it is customary to placate gods of this sort. The bodies they hang in the sacred grove that adjoins the temple . . . Even dogs and horses hang there with men.' This festival would go on for nine days, and by the end of it, scores of human and animal remains would be strung up among the branches.

Gamla Uppsala, then, was once a place of power and worship. It was also, most likely, one of the last real strongholds of paganism in Europe. Here, a distinctly northern mythology held out against the steady expansion of Christianity. According to the medieval Icelandic scholar Snorri Sturluson, the reason the temple on this site had such significance was that it had been built by Freyr himself. And the god – a king, perhaps, deified after death – was buried here beneath one of these mounds.

The archaeological evidence for a temple at Gamla Uppsala is inconclusive, though there were certainly buildings here before the current church was begun, back in the thirteenth century. There is no doubt, however, that the three central mounds were used for burial purposes, as indeed were hundreds, perhaps thousands, of other, smaller mounds in the area, most of which have since been destroyed by agricultural and quarrying activity. Excavations at this site have confirmed that people were cremated here around 1,500 years ago, within large cairns of stone, wood and mud. Because of the intense heat of these cremations, what remains is largely ash and burnt bones, together with a few trinkets, so little can be conclusively determined about the occupants of these tumuli. But it's been suggested that the mounds may indeed be the final resting places of kings – perhaps Ane, Egil and Adils, of the Yngling dynasty – while those graves in the surrounding area contained people of lower status.

H. A. Guerber has contrasted the 'graceful and idyllic' mythology of the 'sunny south' with the 'grand and tragical' ones of the north. 'The principal theme of the northern myths,' she explained, 'is the perpetual struggle of the beneficent forces of Nature against the injurious.' The gods themselves came to represent these various forces, and to personify the motivations, the joys, the troubles and the unfairness of the natural and human world. Like the Inuit concept of sila, this was a religion that directly reflected the place in which it developed. The three gods linked to Gamla Uppsala – Thor, Odin and Freyr – are the best known of the Norse deities. Thor, according to Hilda Ellis Davidson, is 'the characteristic hero of the stormy world of the Vikings'. Son of Odin and of Mother Earth herself, Thor is violent, defiant and extremely strong. His hammer could kill giants, but it could also bring life, and he was considered 'both destroyer and protector'.

Freyr, the supposed founder of the Uppsala temple, was a less contradictory figure than Thor. A bringer of fertility and peace, some version of the god may have been recognised for thousands of years, since the very early days of agriculture. Rites and rituals developed as crops were sown and harvested, and these rituals must certainly have included sacrifice. Life grew from death just as summer grew from winter, and here in the north, where the cycle of the seasons is extreme, the propitiation of a fertility god or goddess would have been of great importance. No matter how warm the summer or how good the harvest, still the cold and darkness and fear will return. It's not surprising that Freyr was worshipped at this time of year; northern religion was surely born in winter.

The third of the Uppsala deities, like Thor, was a complex one. Principally associated with war, Odin was seen as the father of Asgard, the realm of the gods. But that prominence did not make him, necessarily, a 'good' figure, as we might understand that word today. In the sagas and Norse poetry, Odin is sometimes portrayed as untrustworthy and treacherous. He is powerful and wise, certainly, but is more than capable of misusing those qualities. At times, Odin displays older, perhaps pre-agricultural, attributes. Like a shaman, he communicates with the dead and can change his shape, sometimes sending forth his soul in the form of an animal. He employs two ravens – Huginn and Muninn (Thought and Memory) – to keep him informed of events in the world, and his great wisdom is not, like the Christian god's, inherent, but was gained through an act of self-sacrifice. That ordeal, in which Odin hung himself for nine days and nights on the World Tree, Yggdrassil, provides the template for the mass hangings that took place at Gamla Uppsala. Out of suffering would come wisdom, out of death would come life, out of winter would come the spring.

By the time Adam of Bremen was writing, this was already a long-established seat of political and religious power, but it was also a place of tremendous conflict and change. Sweden in the eleventh century was in the middle of a long, difficult conversion from the old religion to the new, a conversion that was not complete until at least one hundred years later, and perhaps more recently still. What we find in Adam's description, therefore, is not just a scene of heathen worship; we see a moment in which two entirely different understandings of the world are painfully coexisting, and in which both are vying for supremacy. Though the man-god Jesus must have seemed familiar to the Norsemen, with his story of sacrifice and rebirth, much else in Christian teaching would have been alien. And in response to the threat of this new faith, it's not difficult to imagine that the rituals of the pagans were becoming stricter, more inflexible and, as Adam's account suggests, more violent. Yet at the same time, both religions were also interacting with and even borrowing from each other. Just as Christianity absorbed some of the old rites, such as the midwinter festival of Yule, so too did the pagans adopt some of the habits of their spiritual opponents. By the tenth century, amulets of Thor's hammer had become quite commonplace across Scandinavia. Wearing such an item would have been an act of open defiance, mimicking the crucifixes worn by Christian converts. It was a battle of symbols as well as ideas.

By the time I'd walked around the three mounds, and down towards the trees, where magpies and jackdaws scrummed among the branches, I was very cold indeed. My cheeks and forehead stung with the chill, and my fingers were numb inside my gloves. Though the sun glowed a fierce orange, it seemed a pathetic effort, and no match for the bitter blows of winter. I stepped inside the church to rest, and to find some warmth, and sat down on a green-painted pew at the back. Upstairs someone was playing the organ, and the sound roared through the building like thunder. Perhaps the organist thought no one was around to listen, for the music was loud and disjointed and unlike anything I'd ever heard in a church before. There were deep blasts of brooding chords, interspersed with what sounded like circus tunes, that together leapt uneasily around the room.

Without warning, the music stopped, and I heard the thud-thud-thud of the organist descending the wooden stairs from the loft. As he emerged at the back of the church I saw he was a man of about forty in a neat, black suit. He moved towards the altar, and was joined by an older woman with dark hair and glasses. Together they began to prepare the church for a service. She set a short crucifix in the centre of the altar, then returned with two candles, placing one on either side of the cross. The lights overhead were dimmed, and those above the altar made brighter. The woman then returned from the vestry, this time with a microphone and cable, and at the back of the church, close to where I sat, she flicked a switch. An electronic clunk said the PA system was now turned on. The woman lit the candles and then shook the match in her hand until it guttered into smoke. She used a wick on a long pole to light the twelve candles sitting high above the altar. The young man hanging on the cross looked down on all of us from his place on the wall, at the front of the church.

One day, perhaps, all of this will be as distant and unfamiliar as whatever it was that happened out there among those trees, one thousand years ago, or within those mounds, five hundred years earlier. One day, the ruins of this building may be as blank and mysterious as the broch on Mousa, which would still have been in use at the time of Christ's death. All of this ceremony, these rituals of allusion and metaphor, will no longer be understood; its meaning will have withered into nothing. How easily we unlearn our codes; how easily a sacred tomb becomes a pile of earth, or a crucifix two planks of wood. Like trying to resurrect the dead from memory alone, our interactions with places like Gamla Uppsala or Mousa will always be thwarted. For the whole is not present in the scraps that remain. It is not present in the stones or the ash or the trinkets or the words. Though we may excavate and examine, take things to pieces and put them together again, so much always will be unrevealed.

Looking back now, my father seems increasingly mysterious to me. I knew him only as a child knows a parent, which is barely at all. And sometimes, when my mother speaks of him, I feel she could be describing a stranger. That awful distance, between the fragments that I still carry and the man that he once was, grows greater each day. The erosion of memory eases grief in time, but is also its own kind of loss. 'I fear for Thought, lest he not come back,' declared Odin, in the poem 'Grímnismál', as he fretted over his two ravens. 'But I fear yet more for Memory.'

The ability to remember and to think, to imagine, are tied tightly together. They are the root of both our salvation and our fear, and the one must be balanced by the other. In the coldest moments of winter we can close our eyes and think back to sunshine. But such memories would be intolerable were it not for the vision of summer to come, and the belief – whether religious or scientific – that it *will* come. Similarly, the pain of loss can be endured only because we can remember the absence of that pain, and so can foresee the day we might awaken whole once more. Rituals are conceived in the darkest hours of winter and of grief, when certainty is hardest to hold on to, and when we imagine not the return of summer or the passing of pain, but the opposite. Through repeated acts of metaphor, fear can be translated into hope, much as memory and imagination can be translated, through acts of metaphor, into writing. Each is a kind of ordering – an effort to forge calm from chaos and meaning from its absence. Each, too, is a kind of faith. My own writing, born in grief, is no exception.

From behind me, three women entered the church, talking in hushed voices. One of them dropped coins into a little box, picked up a candle and lit it, then placed it carefully into a holder nearby. As the congregation began to arrive for the afternoon service, I stood up to leave, pausing for a moment beside four tall clocks near the entrance. Each of these clocks was handsomely made, but none was working. The only explanation for their presence was a notice on the wall, in English, that read: 'One thing is for sure, we are all going to the death in a speed of 60 minutes per hour. This watches (and time) stands still – do the same and give your own time a thought.'

As I stepped back outside, the snow on the Royal Mounds sparkled blue in the bitter light. Every contour had its shadow; every dip and curve in the land was emphasised. Turning back towards the city, I could see the cathedral spires and the pink of the castle in the distance. And as I walked away, on the path through the fields, the church bells behind me began to ring.

*

In their dealings with the outside world, the Nordic countries have all taken slightly different approaches. Of the three that sit upon the parallel, Sweden and Finland have both been members of the EU since 1995, though neither ever joined the European Community prior to that. Between them, Finland has perhaps been most enthusiastic about its place in Europe, embracing the euro right from its launch, while Sweden has chosen to retain its own currency. Norway, on the other hand, has kept out of the EU altogether, yet was a founding member of NATO in 1949, which its eastern neighbours have never joined. Buoyed since the 1970s by its extraordinary oil wealth, Norway has, on the surface, appeared the most aloof of these nations, but this is deceptive. The Norwegian oil fund, worth well over half a trillion dollars, is believed to be the largest stock market investor in Europe. The country may sit outside the EU, but its fingers reach across the continent, and all around the world.

Despite these differences, there's been a great deal of collaboration and integration between the states since the Second World War, and indeed their development through the twentieth century was remarkable in part for the degree to which each chose very similar political roads. Social democratic parties began forming governments and coalitions across the Nordic countries in the Great Depression of the 1930s. Their response to that crisis shaped the region socially as well as economically, and it continues to do so even today. A comprehensive system of welfare, pensions, social housing and healthcare provision, paid for through high taxation and pursued alongside growth and full employment, gradually transformed these nations from economic backwaters into some of the wealthiest in the world. Each of them today boasts an excellent standard of living, combined with low levels of poverty and high levels of income and gender equality. Recent decades have seen liberalisation in their economies, but the Nordic Model, as it's become known, is still looked upon enviously by social democrats the world over. It is still the goal to which others aspire.

But just as many are eager always to laud the social achievements of these countries, others are equally quick to point to a 'dark heart' within the Scandinavian system – a rot that threatens to consume and destroy the positive image projected onto the world. Right-wing extremism is one part of that rot, and its growth in the region has been noted with dismay by liberals across the continent. Ethnic nationalism seems somehow out of place in countries such as these, particularly in Sweden, which until recently had been perhaps the most enthusiastically multicultural and pro-immigration of all European states. There has, undoubtedly, been a change here – a turn towards the right, and a worrying embrace of xenophobic politics among a minority of the population. But ethnic nationalism has been on the rise right across Europe over the past two decades: France, the Netherlands, Austria, Italy, and increasingly the UK, have all seen support for far-right parties increase. The difference in Scandinavia is the sense that such parties ought not to exist there. Such is the degree to which tolerance and social cohesion are portrayed as defining Scandinavian characteristics that current trends have begun to undermine what people outside the region understand it to be. Paradoxically, many Nordic nationalists justify their hostility to immigration by highlighting the threat that multiculturalism poses to the society they have worked so hard to create. By allowing those whose culture is illiberal to come in, they argue – and Muslims are most often the target of this troubling logic – liberalism itself is endangered.

Another development, this time more imagined than real, is crime. In the world of fiction, a parallel Scandinavia, where murder is commonplace, has been growing for decades. It has become a literary and small-screen sensation. Writers such as Stieg Larsson, Henning Mankell, Karin Fossum and others have held up a distorting mirror to their society. Engagement with social and political realities is a distinguishing characteristic of much 'Nordic noir', but the place depicted in these stories is not one that would be familiar to any visitor to the countries in which they're set. Both Norway and Sweden have among the lowest murder rates in Europe, and part of the success of the genre is that very contradiction. Scandinavian crime writing sits at odds with what its readers think they know about Scandinavia; it disfigures and exaggerates the raw material of its location, and is all the more unsettling for that.

It has been said that one single event stands behind the eruption in Nordic crime fiction in recent decades: the assassination of the Swedish prime minister Olof Palme in February 1986. That event was shocking enough at the time, but the fact the murder remains unsolved so many years later has left a wound in the country's politics, and a mystery that refuses to go away. The more time that passes, the more the mystery deepens. In 2011, Norway had its own catastrophic event, which, though very different in character and scale, may yet prove as culturally significant. That the bombings in Oslo and the shootings on the island of Utøya, which together killed 77 people, were carried out by a Norwegian nationalist, who called his actions an attack on Islam, multiculturalism and Marxism, made it somehow all the more shocking. Few could ever have believed that something like this could happen in open, tolerant Norway.

Outside the country, there was a tendency to frame the actions of Anders Behring Breivik within the wider changes in Scandinavian politics and society. Some pointed again to that growing Nordic extremism, and to the region's shift away from its previously-held values, while others argued the opposite: that those very values were at fault, and were somehow responsible for creating the cultural tensions that led to these attacks. Within Norway, however, there was considerable resistance to the idea that these events should be allowed any kind of context. For the crime writer Jo Nesbø, Breivik's self-justification did not deserve to be taken seriously. 'He represents himself and not many others,' the writer argued. 'From a social or political point of view, this is not a very interesting event.'

If crimes such as the massacre in Norway or the murder of Olof Palme are more likely in Scandinavia it may be only because security measures in these countries are less intrusive than elsewhere. And that, many feel, is a risk worth preserving. In the Nordic nations, the possibility of tragedy is considered preferable to the security measures that might be required to prevent it; and that, in the Western world, is a refreshing view. When Oslo's mayor, Fabian Stang, was asked whether this attitude would need to change in the wake of Breivik's attacks, he responded: 'I don't think security can solve problems. We need to teach greater respect.' The country's prime minister Jens Stoltenber echoed that sentiment. 'The Norwegian response to violence,' he said, 'is more democracy, more openness and greater political participation.'

＊

The last time I was in Oslo, I was with Jeff and a small group of other friends. All of us were students in Copenhagen at the time, and were spending our Easter break travelling through Scandinavia. One of these friends was Norwegian, and her parents had graciously agreed to house and feed us all for a night. Sitting down that evening to eat, her father asked each of us in turn where we were from. Alongside Jeff and me, there was a Canadian, an Australian, a Dutchman and a Scot. Her father listened and nodded, occasionally asking questions. When it came to my turn and I answered, 'Shetland', he looked at me and smiled. 'So,' he said, 'you are one of us.' Many Norwegians still cherish the links between the islands and themselves. As a Shetlander, one feels welcomed in this country, like a distant relative come to visit, or an emigrant returned.

On that occasion, as on this one, I felt close to home here. But this time I also felt ready to go back. Wandering the grand streets of Oslo, frozen half to the bone, I found it hard to keep my mind where it was supposed to be. The stinging cold made it difficult to concentrate; it clawed at my face and crackled inside my nostrils. And everywhere I stopped, it seemed, were reminders of other places. In Oslo, the parallel kept turning in on itself. It was no longer a straight line at all, but a tangled, knotted thread that looped this way and that around the world.

Inside the National Gallery, an exhibition of work by Tom Thomson and the Group of Seven brought me back, inevitably, to northern Canada. Those magnificent paintings – of lakes and rivers; of dark forests, empty of people – cried out for reverence. They demanded quiet. For the Group of Seven the landscape was something close to sacred, and they, as artists, were its faithful congregation.

In the University of Oslo's historical museum I was carried back further still. Displayed there were clothing and other artefacts from Roald Amundsen's Arctic expedition of 1903, on which he traversed the Northwest Passage for the first time. On a globe in the exhibition room was marked the route he had taken, following the sixtieth parallel west from Norway, past Shetland, past Cape Farewell, before turning north through the Davis Strait. Amundsen returned from this successful trip in 1906, shortly after his country's independence from Sweden. On future expeditions he was the first to reach the South Pole, thirty-four days ahead of Captain Scott, and he made the first undisputed visit to the North Pole too, by airship, in 1926. Like Tom Thomson, Roald Amundsen would later disappear in the north, but unlike Thomson, his body was never found.

Visiting the Viking Ship Museum on the western edge of the city, I was brought home. It occurred to me there that, while I was in Oslo, Shetland's Viking festival, Up Helly Aa, was taking place. That event – a piece of revivalist pageantry invented by nostalgic Victorians – is one of the big moments in the islands' calendar. Each year, hundreds of men (and only men) march through the streets of Lerwick, with flaming torches held aloft. Some are dressed as Vikings, all Hollywood helmets and gleaming chain mail, while others sport costumes that range from Disney characters to local celebrities. At the end of this procession, a replica longship is burned in a park in the centre of town. And then the men get very drunk, which is perhaps the most authentically Viking thing about Up Helly Aa. Many Shetlanders take the festival extremely seriously; others roll their eyes each time it comes around.

I couldn't remain in Oslo long. I was restless and impatient, and increasingly eager to be moving. Sitting in a café one afternoon, I decided to cut short my trip and go west towards the coast. There I would be closer to the end of the line. In front of me was a mediocre cup of coffee and a few slices of bread and jam that together had cost almost £10. From the speakers, a twenty-second snatch of an Elvis Presley song was playing, stopping, then repeating, over and over. The woman behind the counter didn't seem to notice, and I didn't feel like mentioning it. Each time I looked up she seemed to be staring at me, with a gaze that could have been friendly or suspicious, it was hard to tell. There was something disorientating about the woman: her white hair was too large for her head and her glasses too small for her eyes. I threw back the last mouthful of coffee, stood up and nodded a thank you, then I walked to the train station and booked my seat to Bergen for the following day.

The morning was still gloomy and grey as we headed west from the station, just after eight, through the suburbs and out towards wooded hills and snowy valleys. I fought the urge to close my eyes, and watched instead as we moved through the brightening pre-dawn. At the town of Drammen, the sun was just rising over the water, glowing orange as an ember, though still soft and uncertain around its edges. For a moment it seemed to droop or melt, no longer a circle but an oblong, wilting beneath its own distant heat. In the harbour, steam curled upwards from the sea into the frozen day. I tried to remember a less than flattering Norwegian joke I'd heard once about this town: It's better to have a dram an hour than an hour in Drammen. Or something like that.

Pushing along steep mountainsides, blinking in and out of tunnels, the train threw puffs of ice into the air around us, like smoke belching from an engine. As we climbed higher, the clouds seemed to stoop to meet us. The peaks were all obscured, and everything faded upwards into grey. Even close by, the green of the pines seemed no longer a real colour at all, but instead a new shade of darkness. On either side of the track, each tree bore its burden of snow differently. The conifers were heavy with it – needles and branches arched towards the ground – while silver birches stood delicate as feathers, their leafless twigs a perfect web of white. Up here, the land lay as though in suspended animation. We passed a river, not quite frozen but congealed, as thick and lumpy as custard. In the mountain hamlets, little houses sat with a foot of snow upon their roofs and an exclamation mark of smoke above their chimneys. Flags hung listless from poles. Everything was still except for the train rushing past. From each of these things we were separated by glass and metal, and then by time. In seconds they were gone, a glancing memory, as though perhaps they never quite existed at all. There is much that time takes away and doesn't give back. There is much we wish to keep but lose, just as there is much we wish to lose but can't.

In Geilo, the carriage began to empty as people gathered bags and ski equipment and stepped outside. There, at eight hundred metres above sea level and fifteen degrees below freezing, the sun was just beginning to break through. And further still, at Finse – the highest train station in northern Europe, at more than twelve hundred metres – the sky finally cleared. Snow covered everything there. The buildings were swamped by it. The fences had disappeared. There were no trees and no cars, only quads and snowmobiles, skis and paraskis. From my seat at the window, I squinted out into the dazzling day, where the whole world was winter-lit, and sparkled with anticipation.

*

Bergen must be one of the most picturesque cities in Europe, with its wonky, multicoloured waterfront and precipitous backdrop of mountains. But it is also, certainly, one of the wettest cities. It seems to rain almost constantly from the heavy clouds cradled above the fjords. On this occasion, a steady drizzle covered everything, and the streets were ankle-deep with slush. Everyone stepped slowly and carefully through it, trying to avoid slipping or being splashed by the traffic. But neither was entirely avoidable. Every so often a head would drop down and a pair of legs would come up, accompanied by a yelp. The unfortunate pedestrian would be assisted back to their feet, and everything would continue as before. I spent two damp days exploring the city, then made my preparations to go on.

There are few places in the world where a return journey requiring four buses and three ferries could be planned with confidence for a single day. But in Scandinavia, where public transport is about as reliable as the over-pricing of beer, I didn't doubt for a moment that such a journey would be possible. My destination was the island of Stolmen, a little further south along the coast. It was the last point of land on the sixtieth parallel before it dropped back into the North Sea and then returned to Shetland, and it seemed the most appropriate place to complete my journey before going home. Flicking through the timetables in my hotel room in Bergen, I could see that buses were scheduled to coincide with ferries, and that each connection could be made to fit. The route to Stolmen was rather convoluted, with several changes required, but the return journey was much simpler. A single bus could bring me all the way, including on to the ferry. I could get there and back in a day without any trouble at all, it seemed. I could even have a few hours to wander and explore the island if the weather was good.

The bus drove southwards, past villages and half frozen fjords, in a misty brightness like an English autumn dawn. The sun was uncertain, haze-hidden then bright – a game of celestial hide-and-seek. It seemed a good day to be moving. The route was southwards first, from Bergen to Haljem, where the bus boarded a ferry to Sandvikvåg. From there I took another ferry, northwest to Husavik, on the island of Huftarøy. It was all so easy and effortless, and after only a couple of hours I was most of the way there. At that point, though, the plans I'd made dissolved. There was no drama and no panic, they just dissolved. The connecting bus was due five minutes after the ferry arrived in Husavik, and so I stood and waited at the stop beside the terminal, enjoying the pace of the day. From that stop I had an excellent view of the bus as it appeared, right on schedule, along the road just adjacent to the terminal. I watched it drive along that road, carefully follow each curve, then continue on its way without taking the turn down to where I was standing. It was one of those static moments, like when you shut the door and immediately remember that your keys are on the other side. For a few seconds it seems that, if you regret it hard enough, you might just be able to turn back time. Only the click of that lock separates you from your keys; only a few steps separated me from the correct bus stop on the road above. I stood there doing nothing for several minutes, as though some unimagined solution might just fall from the sky in front of me. The next bus was not for hours – too late to get me to Stolmen and back by the end of the day. I had only two choices: return to Bergen or go on.

I hate hitchhiking. I truly hate it. Perhaps because I only ever do it when absolutely necessary, there is a deep sense of humiliation in me every time I am forced into that position.

And what increases that humiliation, what marks it like a scar upon me, is that I am terrible at it. In the half dozen or so times I've tried to hitchhike in Europe, I've been successful only twice. I have come to believe that somehow my face is unsuitable for the task. It must be a face that people just don't want in their cars, because nobody ever stops for me. They don't stop for me in Shetland and they certainly didn't stop for me in Norway. Following the road west towards where the bus had gone, I stuck out my thumb and smiled at every approaching car. And every car sailed on by, without so much as glance. After an hour or so of this repeated rejection I understood that my choices had been reduced to one. The least humiliating option was to ignore the cars and just keep walking.

I had no idea how far that walk would be, or whether it would get me where I wanted to go in time; and to begin with that absence of certainty only increased my fury. I took every passing vehicle as an insult and every magpie's cackle as a slight. I cursed my journey, and the sheer futility of what I was doing. I cursed myself for my own stupidity. I was looking for a line that didn't really exist, on an island about which I knew nothing. I was striding through a winter afternoon, cold, cross and dejected.

But as the walk wore on, an invigorating acceptance descended on me. I put one foot in front of the other and moved forward. I didn't know when I would get to Stolmen, that was true; but I knew that I would get there. And I didn't know if I could get back to Bergen that day, but I would get back sometime. Walking like that, blocking out the worries and the doubts, I barely noticed the places through which I passed. My thoughts were elsewhere entirely, and yet nowhere in particular. When I arrived in Bekkjarvik after two hours of walking, I was almost as surprised as I was relieved, and when I consulted a timetable at the bus stop by the harbour, I found that a school bus was scheduled to leave the village for Stolmen twenty minutes later. It would give me just over an hour on the island before I had to make my way back to Bergen.

We drove from Bekkjarvik out over the bridge to Selbjorn and onward, over the next bridge, to Stolmen. Red-faced children in snow-suits filled the space with chatter and joy, and every so often a bundle of them would be released into the arms of waiting parents at the roadside. Stolmen was stern and beautiful. Boulders and low trees along the verges stretched out towards rough moorland and crags beyond, and small lakes, distorted by ice. I got off at Våge, at the far south of the island, the end of the road. There was a turning circle at the top of a slope, with a bus shelter on one side and several huts and houses on the other. I stepped out into a thin light and a familiar, salt-ridden breeze.

Once the bus had departed, I could hear no cars, no voices and no machines of any kind – only the intimate whisper of the sea, just a few hundred yards away. It looked like a ghost village, yet at the same time I felt I was being watched from behind a curtain. Some of the buildings, I guessed, might be summer houses, so were probably empty. But others must be occupied. The island has a population of 200, which is not much, but enough.

I had read that Våge was the 'commercial centre' of Stolmen, and I walked back down the road a little way in search of the evidence. So far as I could see, it consisted of a small shop with a petrol pump outside. I went in and browsed the shelves, not wishing to buy anything but just to be there. The shop was well stocked, as stores in out-of-the-way villages usually are, and it gave the impression of a place in which the exchange of words was as important as the exchange of goods and money. Besides me, there were two staff members and two customers. One of them, a woman of about forty with long, curly hair and a thick jacket, was talking quietly and fondly to an elderly man in a fur hat. He seemed to be struggling, as though confused about what he needed, and the woman touched his arm lightly. She was offering suggestions, I thought, and guiding him back towards certainty.

The two women behind the counter then joined the conversation, and each of them spoke in an affectionate, familiar way, oblivious to the roles that elsewhere would define them. Though the words were unknown to me, the tone was not. These were neighbours and members of a community: a connection far deeper than the tenuous bond between buyers and sellers. 'Commercial centre' was a rather inappropriate title for a shop like this, but it was, certainly, a centre.

Wandering those few short aisles, I felt a deep longing to be spoken to in the way those people spoke to each other. By then it was several days since I'd had any kind of conversation with anyone, and I was lonely. But it was more than that. My desire was not really to talk, it was to be known. I wanted to be enclosed and included within that thing of which these people were a part. I wanted to belong, as they belonged, to something bigger than themselves. I missed Fair Isle then, and I longed to go back.

Once outside, I walked briskly towards the sea, over rough ground that crunched with ice at every step. Just above the shoreline I found a rock that looked almost comfortable and I sat down. There was little wind, and the waves unfolded onto the stones with an uncommon tenderness. Towards the west, the tell-tale streaks of a rain shower stained the orange horizon with blue. Everything here was as I knew it should be: the smell of it, the sound of it, the sight. Everything was familiar.

Sitting there beside the sea, two hundred miles from home, I thought back to the traffic that had ventured west from this coast towards my own shores. To the Vikings who had sailed in the eighth and ninth century, and who had made their way ultimately to Greenland and beyond. To the refugees of the Second World War, who were carried in fishing boats and other vessels, in what became known as the 'Shetland Bus'. And then to the oil tanker *Braer*, which left the refinery just north of Bergen in January 1993, carrying 85,000 tonnes of crude oil. She was bound for Quebec in Canada, but made it only as far as Quendale on the south east coast of Shetland, where she hit the rocks and spilled her cargo. It was a few years after my family moved to the islands, and a few miles from the spot where, later, I would find the parallel.

I'd come to Stolmen by following that line around the world. Once there, I had nowhere else to go but home. I'd known all along, of course, that this was a journey with only one possible destination. But faced with that last stretch of water that separated beginning from end, I felt nervous and uncertain. Would the place I was going back to be the same place that I had left? And did I even want it to be? Perhaps I'd expected answers, but I hadn't found any. I'd been left with only questions. Ahead, the sky was like a welt, blue and purple ringed with pink. A crack in the clouds brought sharp fingers of light down onto the blackening waves, and the cold chafed against my face. I sat for ten minutes more, perhaps fifteen, and then it was time to go. I stood and flung a stone into the water, towards Mousa, as though to reach as far as I could towards home, and then I walked away.

HOMECOMING

You can take a ferry north to Shetland almost every night of the year, leaving Aberdeen in the early evening and arriving at breakfast time the following day. It's a convenient, if not always pleasant, way to travel. But on the day I headed home, having flown from Bergen to Scotland, there was no ferry. One vessel was in dry dock undergoing repairs, and the other was leaving Lerwick in the opposite direction. Instead, I booked myself onto the freight boat, which meant a longer and less comfortable journey across the North Sea. But at least it would get me there. And so at three in the afternoon I boarded the *Hellier* together with four other passengers, climbing stairwells and following corridors, each of which reeked of diesel, salt and cold metal.

As the boat shuddered away from the dock an hour later, the five of us were served food: soup, roast beef, chips, cake. A few polite words were shared, but no one was very interested in talking, and as we cleared our plates one after another of us stood up and retired to our separate cabins. The sailing would take eighteen hours, with just a brief stop in Orkney after midnight, and almost as soon as we reached the mouth of Aberdeen harbour the ship began to rock heavily, to an inconsistent beat. The crash of metal on water seemed to shake time loose from its rhythm and drive it forward, confidently, into the night.

Unlike flying, when the moment of arrival is clearly defined – that solid thud as the wheels hit the tarmac – arrivals and departures by sea feel less distinct, more negotiable. To be afloat is to be neither fully detached nor connected, neither here nor entirely there, but suspended, like the boat itself, between elements. I like it. There is something about the pace of the journey that puts me at ease: the sheer slog of it, and the boredom that unravels, wave by wave and roll by roll. Once at sea, I feel almost back where I'm going.

The American writer Harry W. Paige said that 'home is not a place only, but a condition of the heart'. That is to say not that home can be anywhere at all, but that the relationship between person and place is an emotional one. Like being married, being at home is not a passive state. It is a process, in which the heart must be engaged. That is as true for the reindeer herders of Siberia, whose home may be hundreds of square miles, as it is for the inhabitants of a tiny village on a tiny island.

For many people this is not so. Home for them is nowhere in particular. It is the house in which their belongings are kept and in which they go to sleep at night. It extends no further than that. This is the condition of our time. It is a marriage without love, a relationship without commitment. And it is, surely, a kind of homelessness.

But there is another kind of homelessness, too, one which has the opposite effect on its sufferers; and that is the ailment with which, from an early age, I was afflicted. For much of my life I felt myself to be exiled from a home that no longer existed, and which in some sense never really had. In her book, *The Future of Nostalgia*, Svetlana Boym described this feeling as 'akin to unrequited love, only we are not sure about the identity of our lost beloved'. For me that feeling arrived with our move to Shetland, and was compounded by the loss of my father. It became a hole within which I tried, desperately, to find form. Like the north, home is defined in its absence, in the distance between longing and belonging. But, like the north, it is only through intimacy, through love, that it can come to be known.

The landscape that truly shaped me was that of Shetland. This is where I became the person I became. This is where the conflicts that would form me were fought out. That I came to love this place, having once hated it, is strange and yet entirely coherent. It was a process of understanding, familiarity and, I suppose, of forgiveness that brought me back here. In the end, I accepted the centre around which my world was spinning, and I turned towards it.

*

When I woke in the early morning, the *Hellier* was pitching hard, swaying like a drunk heading for bed. We were somewhere around Fair Isle, I guessed, most likely in that stretch of water called the Roost, between the isle and the Shetland Mainland, where tides and currents and winds collide. The water here can be as wild as water ever can be. Something in the cabin was banging each time the ship lurched, a solid clatter against the wall. Hazy headed, I got up to find the cause, groping in the darkness at the end of the bunk. A ladder hung there by its top rail, the bottom half a pendulum swinging in time with the waves. I lifted it from the wall and wedged it at an angle, where it could neither fall nor slide, and I lay back down and closed my eyes.

The lurching became more pronounced then, more violent and uncomfortable. Things that had previously been static were on the move, and each time we rolled to port the curtains remained vertical, inviting a wedge of grey light in to the room. I stood up again and rearranged the cabin, trying to prevent noise and damage. Anything that could move was put somewhere that would stop it; anything that could make sound was silenced. I knew that I wouldn't sleep again, but at least I could lie in peace, rocking almost comfortably through the final miles, until we docked in Lerwick on a dull, wet morning. It was a day much like any other day, except my journey around the world was complete.

It was while living in Fair Isle that I began to write this book. My fixation on the parallel and the idea of a journey around it had never gone away, and there on the island I realised that I might finally be able to achieve it. I abandoned the novel I'd started months earlier, but the ideas that had grown within that book spilled over into this one. What was most important in making this journey seem possible, though, was that I recognised and welcomed, for the first time, my destination. To travel around the sixtieth parallel was ultimately to return to Shetland. Going away was possible, then, because coming back was desirable.

When I set out, I had no idea what I hoped to find, I just wanted to go. Curiosity, restlessness and homesickness: those were the things that had set me on my way, and those were the things that kept me going. Perhaps, somehow, I hoped to satiate those urges, as though by following the parallel to its end I could return settled and content. But things are never quite that simple.

During my travels, I met people who *were* settled and who *were* content. Some had only ever lived in the place where they were born; they were shaped and defined by those places. Others had left one home and found another, in which they felt a deeper sense of belonging. Jeff in Alaska, Ib and Jacques in Fort Smith: I admired their certainty, and their commitment to the places they'd chosen. It was a commitment that, in each case, was renewed and reinforced by engagement, in thought and in action.

But along the parallel there were also those – past and present – who'd been estranged: political and religious exiles; indigenous people whose cultures had been undermined. And perhaps in the north estrangement is more pronounced than elsewhere. For in the north, landscape and climate are uncompromising. They demand, of those who stay there, ways of living that are native to the place. And though it's increasingly easy to ignore such demands, wherever you choose to be, estrangement is never without cost.

*

A few months after I completed the journeys described in this book, something happened to me. It would not be helpful, perhaps, to put a name to it here, for such afflictions always feel distant from the labels we give them. It was, anyhow, a crumbling of certainties and a steady erosion of things I had expected to stay whole. An overwhelming sense of disorientation struck me then, and I felt myself sinking, much as I'd sunk to my knees on that day beside the window, sixteen years earlier. I don't know whether the ending of my travels was the trigger for what happened next, though I can't fully untangle the two things in my mind. Somehow my return seemed to bring me back to the very point at which I'd begun: to grief and to loss and to an absence of direction. Whatever the immediate cause, the result was a year in which I could barely write, and several months when I couldn't work at all. It was a year in which I left yet another house, and a partner who cared for me very much. Turned inward as I was, I lost friendships I didn't want to lose. I felt plagued, in that time, by a darkness I'd not known since my teenage years, and by a hopelessness I thought I'd long left behind.

The most surprising result of this period of sadness and confusion was still to come, however. Since returning from Prague ten years before, I'd been certain I would remain in Shetland. I was stubborn in that certainty, and critical of those friends who, as I saw it, gave in to the appeal of elsewhere. The urge to move comes and goes, I'd told them. You just ride it out and commit to home. Yet at the end of that year, as I began to emerge from beneath my own shadow, I left Shetland and moved south. I left Shetland and I began, once again, to write. In *The Idea of North*, Wally Maclean declared that 'You can't talk about the north until you've got out of it.' And perhaps he was correct, for in those months after leaving I found myself able to complete this book. I understood, finally, what I had to say.

There are moments in life that are remembered quite differently from all other moments. They are replayed and replayed and replayed, as though in doing so the story might turn out differently. But it never does. The story always ends the same. The car always rumbles out of the car park, and it never comes back. I was sixteen when my father died, and I've lived just over half my life without him. In another sixteen years I'll be older than he ever came to be. I couldn't decide the ending on that day; nor could I change it later. But this story is different. Sixty degrees north is a story whose ending I chose.

When I look back to the beginning, to that little boy beside the window in Lerwick, dreaming his way around the sixtieth parallel, I feel sorry for him. He is lost, grief-stricken and alone; or at least he thinks he's alone, which is almost the same thing. If I could, I would reach out to him and take him by the shoulders. I would tell him that one day he will feel whole again. I would tell him that, impossible as it may seem in that moment, he will find his way home.

Index

Acknowledgements

Peter Davidson offered me encouragement when all I had was an idea. He read the earliest chapters and patiently guided me in the right direction. Without his kindness this book would probably never have been written.

During my travels the following people were particularly helpful and hospitable: Rie Oldenburg in Narsaq; Hilary LeRoy-Gauthier, Shawn Bell and Sam Stokell in Fort Smith; Eva Meyer and Maria Jarlsdotter Enckell in Mariehamn; and especially Jeff and Cassandra Raun in Anchorage.

Numerous friends assisted me in one way or another, but Jordan Ogg, Amy Liptrot, Martin MacInnes, Rob Duncan, Ruth Cockshott and Charlene Storey all deserve particular mention. So too do my friends at Nice 'n' Sleazy's acoustic night in Glasgow, who helped me through the last months of writing with their fine company and songs.

Thanks to my agent, Jenny Brown; to Esther Woolfson for her invaluable input; to Gavin Francis; to my editor, Tom Johnstone; and to everyone at Polygon/Birlinn. Thanks also to Creative Scotland, the Scottish Book Trust, Emergents, Shetland Arts and the Arts Trust of Scotland.

I began writing this book while living in Fair Isle. My love for that place and that community will last a lifetime, as will my gratitude towards people there. I felt truly at home on the isle, and still do, in a way that I have never done anywhere else; and my understanding of that crucial word – home – which is at the heart of this book, was shaped by my time there.

Thanks, finally, to my family, for putting up with me.

Author's Note

Three people quoted in this book were unaware that our conversations might be published. I have therefore changed their names.